Mulberry and More

PATRICK WATSON

Copyright © 2022 Patrick Watson.

All rights reserved. No part of this book may be reproduced, stored, or transmitted by any means—whether auditory, graphic, mechanical, or electronic—without written permission of both publisher and author, except in the case of brief excerpts used in critical articles and reviews. Unauthorized reproduction of any part of this work is illegal and is punishable by law.

ISBN: 979-8-88640-526-2 (sc)
ISBN: 979-8-88640-527-9 (hc)
ISBN: 979-8-88640-528-6 (e)

Because of the dynamic nature of the Internet, any web addresses or links contained in this book may have changed since publication and may no longer be valid. The views expressed in this work are solely those of the author and do not necessarily reflect the views of the publisher, and the publisher hereby disclaims any responsibility for them.

One Galleria Blvd., Suite 1900, Metairie, LA 70001
1-888-421-2397

CONTENTS

Introduction 1
Dieppe-a Prelude? 3
Problems and Solutions 10
Supplies and Strategy 19
Mulberry-a Solution? 42
Getting Mulberry Afloat 80
The American Mulberry 93
The British Mulberry 107
The D-Day Landings 118
The Taking of Cherbourg 162
The Rest of the Story 173
Appendix 1 A Partial List of Gooseberry Ships 183
Appendix 2 Tiger 188
Appendix 3 Fortitude 189
Appendix 4 Red Ball Express 191

INTRODUCTION

There have been numerous books and articles written concerning the invasion of Normandy in June 1944. Somewhat surprisingly, there is one facet of that action that seems to have been largely overlooked or even dismissed in many of them. That would be the revolutionary *Mulberry* harbor. An idea so far outside the realm of conventional thinking, that even today it seems almost incredible that it was completed in time. To have designed, completed and delivered such a complex project in a matter of months, borders on the unbelievable.

When I began looking for a project for my next book, I wanted something unique. Something that hadn't been covered and recovered in the thousands of books concerning what is probably the most studied conflict in human history, World War II. When I stumbled onto *Mulberry*, I knew that I had found what I was looking for.

Researching the story was even more daunting than I had anticipated. The few references available on the subject contained so many conflicting versions of numerous events that I sometimes doubted that anyone actually knew what had happened. There were "facts" that no one seemed to agree on. There wasn't any way to form a consensus on many points, so I chose the one that seemed the most logical to myself. So it follows that if there are any errors in this work, they are mine and mine alone.

The heart of this story is naturally the *Mulberry* harbor itself. The *Mulberry* concept came into being in an effort to alleviate a critical problem for the Allies in their initial landings to liberate Continental Europe. It's the same problem that has hounded men since they first began making war on one another, the need for supplies to sustain the fighting forces. There are seemingly never enough. There can be no doubt that it is not the first thing that comes to mind when the subject of war arises, but it may well be the most important. It is the matter of supplies, or logistics as it more commonly known in military circles that enables military action to be sustained. The Allied commanders realized this as well as anyone. *Mulberry* was merely one of the possible solutions to their supply dilemma, but it is the one upon which we will focus.

Originally, I had thought that the completion of the *Mulberry* harbors would be the end of the story. But, after concluding that portion of the project, it still felt unfinished. The logistical issues which were the reason for *Mulberry's* existence weren't resolved until long after the Allies had advanced beyond the borders of Normandy. Rather than leave the story incomplete, I decided to expand the story beyond *Mulberry*, thus the title *"Mulberry and More"*.

The accounts of the American airborne and seaborne landings on the Contentin Peninsula are included to maintain continuity between completion of *Mulberry* and the taking of the port of Cherbourg, Cherbourg being the next step in the supply line that the Allies were trying to establish.

The more I delved into those operations on the Contentin Peninsula, the more I realized that I suffered from an affliction that I am certain affects many others. I have studied World War II for more than 40 years, but it was such a huge conflict that I had gradually lost sight of the trees for the forest. Not until you focus on one specific segment do you realize how little you really know about the war. It was such a huge conflict that even after a lifetime of study, students of the war will find that they have just scratched the surface. I hope that the section on the relatively unknown details surrounding the taking of Cherbourg will encourage others to investigate some of the lesser studied actions that took place during the war. Possibly they will even write a book. If so, I look forward to reading it.

DIEPPE-A PRELUDE?

Dawn had not yet broken on the morning of August 19th 1942 and an Allied naval force was slowly approaching the port of Dieppe on the coast of France in a bold experiment. By day's end, it was hoped that it could be determined whether the Allied plan for an invasion of France was feasible or not. Unfortunately, they were about to find that it was in need of some serious revision.

One of the most serious issues that needed revising was the part that related to the capturing of a seaport. The Allied high command had long appreciated the need for an actual harbor. They couldn't ignore the necessity for proper facilities with which to unload the vast quantities of supplies needed for their armies to survive, much less go on the offensive. What they had to determine was how best to acquire it.

A major seaport was essential for final victory, but until it could be attained alternatives had to be found. It was hoped that interim facilities (i.e. smaller and thus more lightly defended ports) could be secured by direct assault. If those could be quickly captured, it might just be possible to prevent some of the demolition for which the Germans were justly known. If the port facilities required major repairs, it would naturally delay their use. The more intact their objective was at the time of its capture the better. That was their plan, now they had to find out if it would work.

The decision had been made that the idea had to be tested before the planning for the actual invasion began. That was the primary reason for the upcoming operation. It had to be determined if it was possible to attain their goal with the quick, but often costly and always unimaginative tactic of the head-on attack or if something a bit more subtle and creative was required.

Dieppe had been chosen as the objective due to its proximity to Britain, as well as the mistaken belief that it was lightly defended. In one of its previous incarnations the plan for the assault on Dieppe was known as *Operation Rudder*. That plan had the town being taken in a pincer maneuver. It was eventually discarded and replaced by *Operation Jubilee*. The intention now was to land the main assault forces on the beaches directly in front of the town with Commando units neutralizing German fortifications on the flanks. They would then, hopefully, seize control of the harbor and the surrounding area. Once they had accomplished that, they would set about destroying the port facilities and capturing approximately 40 German landing craft that were reportedly in the harbor. Then they would withdraw back aboard their ships and return to Britain. If everything went according to plan, the ground forces would spend no more than 15 hours on French soil.

This was not to be an invasion, merely an experimental raid to verify an idea. Expectations were not high, but with such limited goals hopes for a successful action were. It had been originally intended that the assault would take place in June, but due to a variety of problems that had arisen, mostly weather related, it had been postponed and then finally cancelled.

After the postponement, mission security had all but disappeared. By the time it actually took place in August, the operation had become common knowledge throughout the British countryside around the bases where the troops were stationed. The first time the troops had been briefed on their assignments, loaded aboard their transports and then returned to their billets after the postponement, the word was out. With the failure to confine the individual soldiers to their bases, that was almost inevitable.

It is generally in the nature of soldiers that when it's allowed and sometimes when it's not, to head for the nearest bar after their day is done. After imbibing a couple of their favorite beverages, they naturally begin talking about their work. Even if the recipient of that conversation wasn't a German agent, the gist of it could be passed on until such a person did hear it. It wouldn't have been reasonable to consider confining the troops to their bases for the length of time that we are talking about, but every soldier in the know that was allowed to wander the countryside increased the risk for everyone involved.

This possibility of security leaks was one of the factors that finally led the British High Command, in mid-July to finally cancel the operation. Many of those senior commanders had been less than enthralled with the plan for the raid from the first. They had never felt that the possible rewards justified the risks in attacking Dieppe. Now it was off the table and no longer an issue, or so they thought.

It was at this point that Lord Louis Mountbatten and his Combined Operations staff had stepped in. With the strong support of Churchill, they decided to go ahead with the assault on their own.

Combined Operations had been formed earlier in the war to carry out what were essentially hit and run raids on the German forces along the coastal areas of Western Europe. Since the Germans had chased the Allies into the English Channel two years before Combined Operations had provided one of the few offensive bright lights for the British. But no matter how much their activities raised the morale of the British civilian population their forays into German territory were largely dismissed by established military authorities as merely headline grabbing junkets that might alert the Germans to any deficiencies in their defenses. It would have only been human nature on their part to have wanted to increase their prestige and standing within the military community with a success on a larger stage. This was to be their chance and they weren't going to risk losing it. They would have fought tooth and nail to retain their shot at the big-time. Churchill's motives for continuing to support the operation were in the main, political. Although he was known to have an over-inflated opinion of his own military acumen, in this case however he based his position in the field of politics, an area in which he was much more qualified.

One of his key concerns was the Canadian government. They had delivered their best available unit, the 2nd Division, to Britain in 1940.

The 2nd had been sent to fight the Germans, but for two years it had performed the same duties as much of the British Army, it had trained and trained, and then trained some more. And in that time it had never left the shores of Britain and had never fired a shot in anger.

As a member of the British Commonwealth, Canada was under a certain obligation to support the Mother Country. However, it did retain enough independence so that Britain had to tread lightly to avoid losing what amounted to a voluntary contribution.

When Canada had made the decision to send its best troops to fight the Germans, it was enjoying the luxury of a neutral ocean to its west. That was no longer the case. The situation had changed drastically by 1942. The Japanese had turned the placid Pacific into an active war zone. Japanese forces were already sitting in the Aleutians off Alaska. Canadians could no longer be complacent about their western border. In those first days of the Pacific war, it was feared that the enemy might appear anywhere, even on Canadian soil. Phantom Japanese fleets were constantly being sighted all along the west coast of North America. The chance that one of these imaginary armadas could actually exist kept both the Canadian and the American governments in a state of near panic.

The overwrought citizens and government of Canada were more than a little concerned about the possibility of a Japanese invasion. The government was constantly being bombarded with demands from its citizens that it do more to bolster the defenses along the Pacific coast. The problem was that there were not enough soldiers to do the job. One more division, in reality didn't have the man-power to make much of a difference, but when that division was sitting in Britain instead of sitting in bunkers overlooking the Pacific, it galled many Canadians. If the British weren't going to utilize their best soldiers, the population of Canada was clamoring to have them back to defend their homeland.

Another factor might have been that Canadian troops were volunteers. They had signed up for combat, not to be garrison forces in Britain. There was always the possibility that they might demand to return to their homeland where they could be performing the same functions that they were in Britain but be closer to their own homes.

They had volunteered to fight Germans. For the past two years they had spent their time fighting each other. If they weren't going to fight Germans many would rather be at home.

It could have appeared to the British government that if they didn't justify the Canadians troops' presence in Britain, they could quite possibly lose their services.

There was an additional political problem that Churchill had to deal with. The Western Allies were under intense pressure from the Soviet Union to prove their commitment to the war against Nazi Germany and create a "Second Front". It was obvious to one and all that the Russians were indeed doing the bulk of the fighting and dying in the war up to this point, something even Churchill couldn't deny. That situation had to change.

Soviet Premier Joseph Stalin was certain that that he knew the plan of his "allies" to the west. If he and Hitler were to devour one another, then it would leave the world to America and Britain. In this case, it wasn't just Stalin's famous paranoia running rampant; Churchill for one would not have shed a tear if such an event had actually occurred.

In the meantime, Stalin had to be convinced that the West was not hanging him out to dry. He had to be persuaded that they were as willing to risk spilling American and British blood as they were that of the Soviets. It was hoped that the experiment at Dieppe would do just that.

Again, as so often happened during the war, Stalin was casting his shadow over the plans of the British and the Americans. The need to keep him involved in the war was a constant and overriding concern for both Churchill and Roosevelt. The fear that Stalin would conclude a separate peace with Hitler and leave them to fight the German juggernaut alone undoubtedly cost them many sleepless nights. Perhaps the Dieppe Raid would convince Stalin that the West was serious about helping him defeat Germany, then again, perhaps not.

If that was the hope, then it was in vain. Stalin was not to be impressed with the sacrifice of a couple thousand unfortunate Canadians. Not when he was losing more than that almost every day the war continued. He wanted a Second Front, not an inconsequential raid.

So, on the morning of the 19th approximately 5,000 men, including units of the British Commandos and the American Rangers prepared to land on the beaches at Dieppe, no matter what the consequences. As so often happens during war, it was a combination of political and military expediency that decided the fate of men.

A final nail would be driven into the coffins of many of those men when the ships carrying them encountered a German convoy just off the French coast. There is some disagreement among historians as to whether the ensuing battle further alerted the German defenders ashore or not. Those defenders had already been placed on invasion alert, but the battle off-shore must have gotten their attention. When the assault force landed, it would be in the face of a fully prepared defense. The outcome had been all but determined by the time they began boarding their landing craft off-shore, but they had their orders and they carried on with their mission. That mission would cost them 3,829 casualties.

The decision to continue the attack against an alert and defended position should call into question the judgment of those responsible, in particular Lord Louis Mountbatten who was the commander of Combined Operations. Mountbatten, known as "Dickie" by his detractors as well as his friends, should have included some flexibility in the plan that would have allowed local commanders to adapt to any changes in the situation.

However, in his defense, flexibility was not a common virtue within the British military. When a master plan was received from on high, it was not to be modified. In the American military, operational plans tended to resemble more of a general outline. The British on the other hand were in the habit of issuing strict guidelines which were to be followed to the letter.

In line with this philosophy, it would follow that the onsite commanders would be hesitant to shoulder the responsibility for altering any portion of the operation. But, the unexpected naval battle should have set off an alarm bell in someone's head. If it did, no one admitted to hearing it. Someone in a position of authority needed to show the initiative and have the moral courage to halt the attack when the element of surprise had been lost. It takes a courageous man indeed to risk his career and disobey the orders of his superiors and they may have felt that they could no more stop it than they could a speeding locomotive, but it was part of their job to try.

Whether it was the fear of the potential wrath of a superior or simply a denial of their duty to the men under their command, it didn't matter. Those men, for whom they were responsible, were now on an almost certain suicide mission and no one was going to risk their career to try and stop it.

The actual battle for Dieppe and the mistakes made there are topics that could fill an entire book on their own and have done so in many cases. So, in an effort to limit the scope of our story, we will have to leave the actual combat portion of that historic and largely forgotten battle until another time.

Winston Churchill would later call the action a "successful reconnaissance". Those who didn't return from the shores of France that day may have preferred a somewhat different term for the costly fiasco that was the "Dieppe Raid".

PROBLEMS AND SOLUTIONS

If there was an upside to the Dieppe disaster for the British, it was that it gave them a means of controlling their impetuous Allies, the Americans. Many senior American commanders had their hearts set on invading France in 1942. They pinned their hopes on what was known as *"Operation Sledgehammer"*. *Sledgehammer* had originally been conceived as an emergency measure to relieve pressure on the Soviets if their situation became critical in 1942. It was thought that a landing by Allied forces on the coast of France would force the Germans to transfer forces from the Eastern Front to defeat it.

The more the Americans had looked at *Sledgehammer*, the more it began to emerge as a viable solution to winning the war. They felt that it could be the first step in the journey to the liberation of Continental Europe and eventually, the end of the war. There was also the hope that it would pull the British away from their planning conferences and back into action. The British, for their part, were just as firmly convinced that it would be shear recklessness to attempt any major landings in France at this stage of the war.

This theory is in no way implies that the British intentionally sacrificed the Dieppe landing force merely to convince the Americans of the folly of an early return to France. There can be little doubt though, that after the action when they were trying to find something positive to discuss; the possibility of the negative results slowing down their aggressive allies must have arisen.

Admittedly there were real lessons to be learned from the failed operation, which has been termed by some as a rehearsal for D-Day. "Rehearsal" may be stretching the point a bit. Several far more important amphibious operations (i.e. North Africa, Sicily, Salerno and Anzio) would take place before the actual D-Day landings in 1944. Those would prove to be far more beneficial to learning about the do's and don'ts of a major landing. Dieppe was but the first small step in learning the basic tenets of landing on a hostile shore. However, the trials and tribulations experienced there would prove to be somewhat useful in the planning stages of "*Operation Overlord*" two years later, but a rehearsal?

Many of the lessons learned at Dieppe would seem so obvious at first glance that it is hard to imagine that professional military men couldn't have come to the same conclusions without the loss of so many lives.

Among the revelations that came to light was that they needed to tighten security for any future operations. The forces destined for the Dieppe operation had been free to come and go from their billeting areas as they pleased, even after the many delays. It would be very different two years later on D-Day. On that occasion, operational security was much more efficient and professional.

In 1944, in contrast to the situation two years earlier, the assault forces were quarantined within specific areas in the south of Britain, in what were called "sausages". This expression was in actuality a description of their resemblance to that particular meat product when they were viewed on a map. Within those sausages were hundreds of Allied intelligence agents who were on the lookout for possible German agents. They were also alert for any careless talk by members of the Allied forces concerning *Operation Neptune/Overlord*.

Even the British civilian population was involved in maintaining the secret of the operation that was so vital to their very existence. Somewhat ironically, the situation in southern Britain began to resemble to that in Nazi Germany. Since Hitler's rise to power, Germany had become a virtual police state. Any statement or opinion expressed in public, or in private for that matter, could well be reported to the authorities. Even immediate family members were informing on one another.

For the most part, the paranoia never reached such extremes in Britain, but local police stations were indeed inundated with reports of "suspicious" activities committed by fellow Brits. The ease with which British society began to resemble that of Germany is more than a little interesting.

The stringent official security blanket didn't just cover local citizens and the men who would be actually crossing the Channel. Those who resided at Supreme Headquarters Allied Expeditionary Force headquarters in London were also under close scrutiny. There were several cases of senior officers who were accused of security breaches being severely disciplined. In many instances, those officers were sent home in disgrace. Their military careers ruined for some indiscretion that would probably have been overlooked on other less important occasions.

The Allies also felt as though they had dealt with communications issues that had arisen during the Dieppe operation. In actuality they hadn't gone far enough. Their plan apparently was to just to send additional radios ashore with the landing forces. They didn't seem to appreciate the fact that they were still dealing with electronic equipment that was highly susceptible to water and shock damage. The radios of that era were just too sensitive and fragile. They could send in all the radios they wanted, but once those radios got wet or were damaged in a parachute drop, they were just so much dead weight. And damaged they would get; it was an amphibious/airborne operation after all. The equipment was inevitably going to endure many situations for which it wasn't designed.

With all the bright and inventive minds available, it would seem that someone on the side of the Allies could have come up with an idea to improve the durability of the vital and potentially life-saving radios. They didn't, and men would die in Normandy as they had at Dieppe because not enough thought had been given to the vulnerability and limitations of their communication systems.

There was one pathetic attempt to improve the communications situation between the air and ground forces. Colored smoke, as well as orange panels that were to be laid out on the ground were provided to the ground forces. The intention was to enable Allied aircraft to identify Allied positions from the air and hopefully prevent attacks on friendly troops. In today's parlance, a loss attributed to this "friendly" fire is known as fratricide. In some cases, they worked, and in many they did not. There was no way to control the smoke. It went where the wind sent it. If that was back over the Allied lines, then so be it. There was no direct line of communication to inform the airmen of the situation. The panels were often placed improperly by well-intentioned, but poorly trained Allied soldiers. Sometimes, the Germans stole the panels and intentionally placed them in the wrong location.

Another lesson of the Dieppe operation was that heavier and more effective naval gunfire support was essential for any hope of a successful landing. At Dieppe the largest naval vessels available for direct support had been destroyers. These craft, armed with relatively small 5-inch cannon were sufficient for dealing with light fortifications, but were completely inadequate for eliminating the well-built positions the Germans had constructed around Dieppe. Although Mountbatten had requested the services of a battleship or at least a cruiser, the British Admiralty had refused. They weren't willing to risk any of their precious larger warships in such confined waters. It would be far easier to condemn this action, or lack of it by the Royal Navy if the pre-attack intelligence reports submitted by Combined Operations itself hadn't badly underestimated the strength of the German defenses. Even though Mountbatten had asked for more firepower, he apparently didn't feel that it was essential for success. He didn't push the matter.

When the time came to plan the actual pre-invasion bombardment for the 1944 landings in Normandy, this was one Dieppe lesson that was either disregarded or forgotten. Larger warships were indeed available for *Neptune/Overlord*, but they weren't fully utilized. This was largely the fault of the Army commanders. Unlike most of the leaders in the Navy, those of the Army were less than convinced of the effectiveness of naval bombardment. Many in the Army deemed the element of surprise to be far more crucial than any possible benefit that might be derived from an extended shelling of the German positions. The main concern expressed by those holding such opinions was that if the shelling began too soon the German defenders would have time to respond and could rush reinforcements to the threatened area.

This trepidation felt by the leaders of the landings might have been more understandable if the pre-invasion bombardment had been scheduled to last for days or weeks, as was often the case of assaulting islands in the Pacific Theater. But it wasn't. That was never considered a serious option.

It had been realized early in the initial planning, that in contrast to attacking an island, they were attempting to establish a foothold on an entire continent. It would have been infinitely easier for the Germans to reinforce their positions if they received advance warning of an invasion than it would have been for the Japanese on the islands of the Pacific. The Americans in that theater could safely commit to extended bombardments without fear of radically changing the local tactical situation. In the Pacific the American strategy was based on having complete control of the seas around their objectives. It would be almost impossible for the Japanese to move any substantial reinforcements to a threatened island outpost, no matter how much warning they had. The situation for the Germans in Normandy would be far different. They could not be completely cut off from their forces in the invasion area. With advanced warning, there would always be the possibility of major German units being moved into the threatened positions.

The question is what effect a few more hours of shelling would have made to the reactions of the German defenders, probably not much in view of the sluggish and confused response actually exhibited by the Germans during the initial landings. Even later on the day of the landings when Hitler and his subordinates were informed of the invasion they failed to act as the Allies had feared they would. For weeks they held onto the belief that Normandy was not the primary invasion.

Possibly it was hoped by those same senior Allied officers that a planned attack by the heavy bombers of the American 8th Air Force immediately prior to the landings at *"Omaha"* beach would make up for any shortcomings on the part of the naval bombardment. Unfortunately, if that was so, it was faith misplaced. When the Air Force failed in its assigned mission to fill the gaps in the pre-landing destruction of the

German defenses, it would again be the combat infantryman who would pay the price for the questionable calls made by their superiors.

The timing of the tides was another factor in determining the length of the naval shelling prior to the landings. The optimum tidal conditions for landings during the time period chosen were only present soon after sunrise. The opening salvos of the bombardment could have been fired before dawn to compensate for the limited daylight available before the landings, but apparently that wasn't considered necessary by the planners. Granted that the observation of specific targets would have been limited by the darkness, but a walking, or rolling, barrage starting at the low water mark and working its way inland would have helped eliminate the anti-invasion obstacles and the anti-personnel and anti-tank mines which caused such chaos among the assault forces.

Also, it had been decided that as the bombardment as planned was probably incapable of destroying the larger the German fortifications. It would serve to neutralize them instead. A general shelling of the area would have a detrimental effect on the defenders themselves, as well as on the smaller and less fortified German positions behind the beaches. In the end, these were mainly the sites that suffered most from the naval shellfire anyway. But if that was the case then why not start the bombardment during the hours of darkness instead of waiting for daylight to expose the specific targets that they weren't really trying to eliminate anyway.

The 40-minute bombardment that was finally allotted to the American beaches seems almost ludicrous. It may have helped the morale of the soldiers aboard the landing craft headed towards the assault beaches, but that would have only lasted until the ramps of their assault craft dropped. That's when they would receive a face full of machinegun fire from the largely intact German defenses.

It was almost a case of why bother? If it hadn't been for the superlative close-in fire support supplied by destroyers during the initial landings, the Navy's contribution could be considered minimal at best. For the most part, the Navy might as well have stayed in port for all the good they accomplished during their "pre-invasion bombardment". The larger warships would indeed prove their worth later in the campaign when they served as long-range artillery for the ground forces, but during the actual landings, the "pride" of the Navy just took up space off-shore. Again, this was not the fault of the commanders of the Navy, but those of the Army who valued surprise above all else.

An interesting, and largely futile, attempt was made by the planners to provide additional fire support for the landings. It was to be supplied by rocket-firing small craft, as well as Army artillery pieces that were positioned to fire shore-ward while still aboard the landing craft that were carrying them ashore. Unfortunately, the rockets proved to be a major disappointment. For all their smoke and noise, they were found to be wildly inaccurate, with most falling well short of the beach. The Army cannons mounted aboard the bouncing landing craft were not much more effective. An interesting scheme, but not very well thought out.

As for command of the air over the assault beaches, that was one lesson that had been taken to heart in the halls of London. When D-Day finally arrived, the Supreme Allied Commander, American General Dwight Eisenhower, could confidently assure his forces that if they saw an aircraft overhead they need not worry, it would be friendly. He wasn't far off-base with that guarantee. Other than a few what could be considered relatively minor attacks, the German Luftwaffe would be all but nonexistent on this critical day in the history of the Third Reich.

Another possible benefit the Allies may have derived from their defeat at Dieppe was its psychological effect on the German High Command. The invaders had been beaten so handily that it led the defenders to become slightly over-confident in their ability to repulse any future attacks. In fact, many, including Hitler himself, would afterward harbor doubts that the Allies would even attempt another landing at all.

Another serious issue that arose during the Dieppe operation was that very few of the tanks that were to have provided close support for the infantry had even reached dry land. Those that did were for the most part quickly isolated and destroyed by the German defenders. This would lead to the creation of a series of specialized armor, or what were more commonly referred to as "Hobart's Funnies".

As mentioned earlier, probably the most important thing the British and Americans drew from the whole affair at Dieppe was that the Germans were going to make any attempt to capture a seaport a long and bloody affair. The direct assault that had been contemplated before Dieppe was completely out of the question.

The Germans, for their part, would build defensive positions along the most likely invasion beaches to slow down the Allies and to buy time for their inevitable counter-attack. But they knew that a seaport was the key. Their primary goal was to prevent the Allies from gaining control of one.

Without a proper seaport there was no chance of an Allied invasion succeeding. The Allies would in all probability secure a beach-head wherever they landed, but if they were unable to resupply their assault forces, they would face another Dunkirk-type evacuation or they would end up providing the Germans with the world's largest self-sustaining prisoner of war camp.

One other far-reaching recommendation came out of the Dieppe operation. On October 12, 1942, it was decided that a permanent naval assault force was needed. It would be responsible for devising equipment and tactics to be used in further amphibious attacks. Its core would consist of the naval force that had gone to Dieppe, even including the commander of that unit, Commodore John Hughes-Hallett. It was to be known as Force "J".

Hughes-Hallett would hold his position until the latter part of 1943 when he was appointed to Headquarters Home Fleet. He was replaced temporarily by Rear Admiral Sir Philip Vian, who left in February 1944 to assume command of the British invasion fleet. Vian was eventually relieved by Commodore G.N. Oliver. Oliver would lead Force "J" when it landed and supported the Canadian 3rd Infantry Division on *"Juno"* beach in Normandy on June 6th.

In learning these valuable, if in many cases seemingly obvious, lessons at Dieppe where the Allied high command had all but destroyed Canada's best available military unit. It had also given itself an embarrassing black eye and had presented the German propaganda machine with a gift that it would make the most of throughout Occupied Europe.

Although the Allies did take something away from the beaches of Dieppe, the operation couldn't answer all the questions concerning D-Day. The long-term goals of the two operations were far different. The action in Normandy was not going to be a hit and run raid. It would be an invasion that was meant to liberate a continent.

SUPPLIES AND STRATEGY

An actual invasion would entail many details that would never arise in a 1-day raid. One of those was the matter of supplies. Resupply had not been an issue at Dieppe. Other than the amount of ammunition and provisions that might be required a single day of hard fighting, there were no other supplies to be concerned with. If the Allies meant to stay in France on their next visit, they would need essential combat materiel in staggering amounts. Literally millions of tons of everything from toothbrushes to tanks had to be delivered and stored.

The Allies would have to overcome countless problems, logistical and otherwise, in their upcoming campaigns. Their path to victory wouldn't be a smooth one, but they would eventually succeed. How much of that success would be due to skill, luck or quality of their equipment will be debated for years to come.

Much of that debate has been instigated by the post-war accounts of German veterans. In the opinion of many of those, it was the amount of ordinance that the Allies were willing and able to expend rather than the abilities of their individual soldiers that won the war. This attitude may have some basis in fact, but it can also be attributed in part to the very human tendency to justify their own shortcomings or mistakes.

When one looks at the "official" numbers it's hard to argue with many of the statements made by the Germans. An Allied infantry division required a minimum of 520 tons of supplies per day to maintain even limited offensive operations. A German division on the other hand needed only 200 tons. But, the "facts" aren't as cut and dried as they first appear.

Upon further study of the supply requirements of the opposing forces, there are major differences that arise. The Allied Armies, for their part were far more mechanized. The German Wehrmacht on the other hand was, even at this late date, still largely horse-drawn. That made the matter of logistics far less complicated for the Germans than it was for the Allies. A German horse could be left to graze in a field at almost no cost to its masters, while the mechanized Allied forces demanded millions of gallons of gasoline for their gas-guzzling vehicles. Each and every gallon of that gasoline had to be delivered to the frontlines by an equally thirsty mechanical beast of burden. The huge amount of that critical and scarce commodity was to constitute a major portion of that disparity in the supply demands of the opposing forces.

The actual number of personnel in comparable units on either side also varied widely. Even at the beginning of the war, a German division had contained fewer men than a similar Allied unit. The numbers had grown even more disparate as the war continued. This was partially due to combat attrition, but also to the fact that the German high command preferred to establish new units rather than replenish older ones. The number of divisions continued to grow even as the number of Germans in uniform declined. In the dream world that was Hitler's headquarters, this fact was often ignored. Grandiose operations were often planned for full-strength units when they were in reality at half-strength or less.

One supply issue the Germans did have in their favor can be realized by simply viewing a map of Europe. The further they were pushed away from the Channel coast, the closer they were to their own supply and production base at home in Germany. Their supply line became shorter with every mile they retreated.

Be all that as it may, there can be no question that the almost overwhelming superiority of the Allied supply situation was a huge factor in the outcome of the war in Europe. It may not have been the ultimate reason for the Allied victory, but it most assuredly didn't hurt.

But all those supplies would be useless if they weren't in the hands of the men fighting at the front. And they weren't going to get there by landing them by hand directly onto the beach. It would have been physically impossible to manhandle the quantities needed. The Allies eventually had to have an actual harbor. It would have had to be of sufficient size to handle the number of ships required. It also had to be fitted with cranes, wharves and warehouses that could only be found in a major seaport. Until that objective had been gained, a temporary solution had to be found.

This need for harbor space was deemed extremely critical by Supreme Commander Dwight Eisenhower. It became one of the main reasons that he was so vehement in his insistence that *"Operation Anvil/Dragoon"* (the invasion of southern France) proceed as originally planned. In his mind, the fact that it would possibly draw German forces away from the main front in northwest France was almost secondary. It was the possibility of gaining the use of the major port of Marseilles on the Mediterranean coast that was uppermost in his mind.

An additional motivation in Eisenhower's mind for the successful completion of Anvil, was his "broad front" strategy. Since he had assumed command of the Expeditionary Force, he had insisted that pressure be applied to the Germans along the entire front. Having the *Anvil* forces join up with his right flank would enable him to have a continuous line from the Swiss border to the North Sea. It would hopefully insure that at no single point would the Germans enjoy a respite that might enable them to move forces to reinforce another area or possibly mount a counter-offensive.

Unfortunately, Eisenhower's theory didn't work out too well. On December 16th 1944, the Germans managed to accomplish exactly what Ike had hoped to avoid. They stripped troops and armor from other fronts and moved them to reinforce one area. That area was the Ardennes forest in Belgium. They then launched a major offensive that is known to history as the "Battle of the Bulge". Although the German attack was beaten back, it did raise questions concerning Eisenhower's strategic abilities.

The British high command had never been in agreement with Eisenhower's strategy of attacking along the entire front. They wanted a spearhead-type offensive by one of the two Allied Army Groups.

Naturally they preferred that the British 21st Army Group be given the assignment. After the near disaster in the Ardennes they felt more than justified in their doubts.

The maintenance of what they considered Eisenhower's ill-conceived broad front strategy was only one problem the British had with the Americans pet project *Anvil/Dragoon*. They also feared that such an operation would draw forces away from the operations in Italy, a campaign near and dear to their hearts. They still hoped to ultimately defeat Hitler by driving through the "soft underbelly" of Europe, rather than confronting his main defenses in the north.

Churchill was so disgruntled with the decision to continue with what had been originally called "*Operation Anvil*" that he continually referred to it as "*Operation Dragoon*". He felt that he had been dragooned, or forced into granting his sanction to an action of which he most definitely did not approve. He used the term so often in official correspondence that it eventually became part of the official title.

In the end, Eisenhower got his southern invasion but not when he wanted it. It was originally to have occurred simultaneously with the landings in Normandy, but the shortage of suitable landing craft forced a postponement until August 15th. Again, the paucity of the menial landing craft would alter the schedule of what the Allies hoped was a war-winning strategy.

In the master plan for the Allied liberation of Continental Europe, the port of Antwerp with its 60,000 tons per day capacity in Belgium and the smaller Channel ports were to have been the ultimate answer to the supply issues for the British and Canadian forces in their portion of the offensive against Germany. But, when the operation to secure Antwerp was bungled by the British 21st Army Group; it threw a monkey wrench into the works. Until the British could utilize the port facilities of Antwerp, they would have to make do with what was left of Le Havre and the smaller and less efficient harbors along the Channel and the North Sea, as well as their surviving Mulberry harbor at Arromanches. The failure to properly secure Antwerp and its approaches would add months to the war. It would also make the possession of Marseilles to the south even more crucial in the eyes of Eisenhower.

The Americans on their right weren't much better off. It had been originally intended that they would be resupplied directly from the United States by shipping that would be unloaded in Cherbourg and the Brittany ports, as well as a man-made facility scheduled to be constructed at Quiberon Bay. For a variety of reasons which will be discussed later, those plans changed.

The Allies were then stuck with a series of makeshift solutions until a more satisfactory answer could be found to their supply problems. One of those was the relatively well-known, but not very cost efficient "Red Ball Express" (See Appendix). They even attempted to supplement their resupply efforts by utilizing aircraft as flying tankers, an even less productive and more wasteful option.

No military operation could be undertaken after the Allies set foot ashore in Continental Europe without first considering where the bullets and fuel were going to come from. There just wasn't enough to go around. More often than not, one action had to be halted or postponed so that another could proceed. The war in Europe would last into 1945, not so much due to resistance on the part of the German Army, but because of the almost unbelievable supply situation that dogged the Allies' every move.

An often-over-looked consequence of the supply issues that the Allies were dealing with was to be felt by the frontline troops when the winter weather finally arrived in northwestern Europe. Due to the shortage of supplies and the vehicles needed to transport them to the front, the Allied high command had to make a decision fill the available trucks with bullets and fuel or winter clothing.

That decision probably wasn't as difficult as it could have been. The majority of senior Allied commanders, as well as many junior ones, felt that the war would be over by Christmas. Such was the state of over-confidence in the Allied high command that General Eisenhower half-jokingly made a five-pound bet with British Field Marshal Montgomery that the war would be over by the holidays. In that case, the warm clothing and overshoes wouldn't even be needed. Unfortunately, Christmas came and went. Eisenhower paid his gambling debt, and the combat infantrymen were still fighting in water-filled foxholes under snowy skies while wearing equipment designed for the milder weather of spring and summer. During the "Battle of the Bulge" in December of 1944, American infantrymen were even reduced to stealing white sheets from civilian homes in Belgium. The stolen sheets would serve as personal camouflage on the snow-covered battleground, personal camouflage that should have been provided by their own supply organization. In several cases unit commanders were actually brought up on charges for these acts, this while those really responsible were sitting safely behind their desks well to the rear. Someone along the line had dropped the ball and once again the ground pounders paid the penalty.

It wasn't only the matter of camouflage that had been mishandled. More than 45,000 of America's finest would have to be evacuated with severe cases of frostbite and trench foot because they had not been supplied with the proper protective clothing. This, while many of their rear echelon comrades were sitting in warm billets back in Paris with so many extra winter parkas and overshoes that they were selling them on a thriving black-market. This isn't to imply that everyone serving in the rear areas was less than honest, but the temptation proved too great for many.

The ranks of the black market in Europe were filled with thousands of American deserters. It is a little-known fact that somewhere between 8,000 and 18,000 unattached American servicemen were wandering the back streets of Europe, many creating mischief of the worst kind. There were even rumors of the American "Mafia" being involved in this very lucrative enterprise.

Millions of dollars worth of gasoline, clothing and cigarettes simply disappeared after they were unloaded off the ships that had carried them from the New World to the Old. The further the frontlines moved away from the denizens of the rear echelon, the more brazen they became. It eventually got to the point where pitched gun battles were taking place in the streets of Paris between the American military police and the black-marketeers. Men were dying at the front while fellow members of the *"greatest generation"* were stealing and selling equipment that might have kept them alive or at least made their miserable lives a little more bearable.

It wasn't just common thievery and corruption that hindered the Allied war effort. The system that had been counted on to sustain the combat units at the front proved to be less than effective, to put it charitably. Whether it was a lack of planning, incompetence or a combination of those and other issues, it provides a sad commentary on the staff work of the Western Allies. Considering the years that were available to the planners of the *"Great Crusade"*, it was indeed unfortunate that more thought wasn't given to the question of supply and demand.

On the American side, the crux of the problem was the Services of Supply branch commanded by Lieutenant General **John C.H.** Lee. It would eventually be based in Paris and was responsible for moving the crucial war materiel from the seaports to the point where it was needed most, the frontlines. It was designated as the Communication Zone or ComZ for short. That unit's failure to perform its mission as required, would contribute greatly to the supply issues that beset the Allied war effort after the breakout from Normandy.

In ComZ's defense, it should be pointed out that the sudden German collapse after the battle for Normandy had caught the Allies off guard. They had expected a slow withdrawal by the Germans to the next defensive barrier, the River Seine. That might have given ComZ time to organize its supply situation.

Their inexplicable failure to have contingency plans in place for such an occurrence could only have been a matter of professional incompetence. One can never expect operations to always proceed according to plan during war. The unexpected must be expected, or at least prepared for.

Lee, known by many as **Jesus Christ Himself**, due to his initials as well as his self-righteous personality, was the head quartermaster for the American European Theater of Operations. Quartermasters throughout military history have acquired a reputation, perhaps undeservedly, of placing their own comfort ahead of taking care of the troops at the front. Lee, as quartermaster for one of the largest military operations in history, was the recipient of possibly more resentment than usually came with the position. From much of what has been written about the man, it would seem that he brought on much of the venom himself.

In September, at the height of the Allied supply crisis, Eisenhower had issued orders that no major headquarters were to be situated in large metropolitan areas. This had been a longstanding policy of Eisenhower's. When he had assumed command of SHAEF, he had ordered that his headquarters be moved out of London to a more isolated location. This move had caused much discontent among his staff but significantly increased its efficiency. This was due in large part to the lack of social distractions that had been readily available in London. He did carry it to an extreme when he finally moved his headquarters to the Continent after the invasion. He chose the somewhat isolated town of Granville as the site. The facility would suffer communication issues until it was finally moved to the Triananon Place Hotel in Versailles outside of Paris in its next and final move.

It might be assumed that Ike's declaration would have included the city of Paris. Lee apparently never got the word, or more likely chose to ignore it. He decided that Paris would serve as a bastion of the rear echelon. He decreed that his headquarters would be established there as soon as possible. By the time Ike heard about the unauthorized move, ComZ was firmly entrenched in Paris with almost 30,000 men. Tens of thousands more would soon follow. Eisenhower, ever the diplomat, chose to tolerate this disregarding of his orders. By the end of the war there would be 160,000 members of the US military living the good life in ComZ's Department of the Seine, which was located in the heart of Paris.

By the first of September, there were sufficient supplies stored on the Continent to support limited offensives by both Allied army groups. The problem was transporting those supplies to the front. That was the responsibility of ComZ. Through a combination of incompetence and an incredible of lack of preparation, they failed to fulfill their obligation to the forces on the frontlines.

By the 2nd of September, the supply situation on those frontlines had become critical. An active Allied division required more than 500 tons of supplies per day to continue operations and in many cases, they weren't receiving it. As a result of the shortages, several divisions had to call a halt to all offensive operations for extended periods of time. In the case of the British, their entire 8th Corps was "grounded" and had to cease any offensive actions. At a time when they should have been pressing the Germans as hard as possible, the Allied armies were being forced to do just the opposite.

Another increasing supply problem for the Allies is often overlooked. As more territory in France was liberated, the heavier the demand on the less than efficient Allied supply system. The logistical demands of the French population had to be met. Indigent food and fuel supplies were not sufficient to support the civilian population in the best of times, so it was up to the British and Americans to make up the difference. After four years of occupation by the less than benevolent Germans, the people of France were in no mood to cut even further back on their consumption now that they were free. The city of Paris alone required more than 2,400 tons of food and fuel every day. Eisenhower had seen this situation coming and had even considered temporarily bypassing Paris in order to postpone this drain on his resources. The French Army commander Charles De Gaulle, the weight of public opinion and a surprise uprising by local Resistance forces caused him to reconsider his plan however.

The British 21st Army Group was no more immune to supply problems than was the American 12th. British commander Montgomery assigned the Canadian 1st Army the task of capturing the small seaports along the coasts of the English Channel and the North Sea. But by the time the Canadians had accomplished their mission the war had in large part moved on. Those harbors were to suffer from the same affliction as the larger ports on the Biscay coast to the west. They were too far from the front. The time and effort expended in moving the supplies the increasing distance to the frontlines were barely justified by the results. Not until the port at Antwerp in Belgium had become fully operational after the first of the year would the Allied supply issues finally ease somewhat.

Of all the shortages that Allied strategy was to suffer, the most critical was that of fuel. The American Third Army alone requested 750,000 gallons of fuel on September 2nd and received a mere 25,390. The next day wasn't much better. They asked for 590,000 gallons and ended up with less than 50,000. Every day the Allies front remained stagnant due to the lack of fuel was another day the Germans could utilize to bring up reinforcements and strengthen their defenses against the Allied attacks.

One of the reasons given to history for the discrepancy in what was requested and what was received by the American armies was that most of the available fuel was being diverted to Montgomery's 21st Army Group. Montgomery was preparing for his upcoming attempt to take the city of Arnhem and to secure a crossing over the Rhine in "Operation Market/Garden". He had convinced Eisenhower that his offensive would shorten the war. Even though it went against his stated strategy of a front-wide offensive, a hopeful Ike had decided to grant Monty the highest priority when it came to supplies of any sort, especially fuel.

Considering Field Marshal Montgomery's past history with the senior American commanders, this must have pleased them no end. American generals Bradley and Patton had their own plans for ending the war, and those most definitely didn't include Montgomery racing into Germany and garnering all the glory. There had been many personality and philosophical clashes between them during previous campaigns in the Mediterranean Theater, as well as in Normandy. Those would continue as long as any of them lived.

During the "Battle of the Bulge" in December much was made of the fact that American fuel dumps holding up to 400,000 gallons of gasoline were kept out of German hands. The numbers sound impressive until it is realized that those "huge" fuel depots wouldn't have supplied even one of the Allied armies fighting on the Continent for a single day. It was important that the Germans didn't capture the fuel that would have enabled them to continue their attack, but the numbers add an interesting perspective to the differing situations of the combatants.

This emphasis on the supply problems of the Allies is not meant to imply that the Germans weren't fighting. They were, and as hard as they possibly could. But, if the Allies had been able to maintain the pace at which they were advancing after they broke out of Normandy, the Germans would not have had the time required to rebuild their forces in the West. The war might have been over by Christmas as everyone on the Allied side hoped.

The Germans themselves had different and more widespread issues in the spring and summer of 1944 to deal with. The war against the Soviets on the Eastern Front was bleeding them dry. Their losses in that theater already numbered more than 2,000,000 men. They were also fighting the Western Allies in what was basically a stalemate in Italy. At the same time their cities and industries were slowly being obliterated by Allied bombers. An Allied invasion of France was all but inevitable, but where, and how to defend against it?

They realized that they couldn't properly defend the entire Channel coast, so they had to defend what they considered the most likely objectives for the Allies. One of those objectives was sure to be a seaport, which would be critical to the success of any invasion.

The Germans had already been forced to spread their forces dangerously thin along the Channel, but the Allies wanted them thinner. The most perilous time for the invading forces was the first few days after the initial landings, before they had time to consolidate their positions. If they could somehow distract the Germans or deceive them into believing that the invasion was to occur elsewhere, so much the better.

It was for this reason that a large part of the pre-invasion planning by the Allies concerned an intricate deception program called "*Operation Fortitude*". The purpose of *Fortitude* was to convince the Germans that the upcoming invasion of France would occur at almost any point other than Normandy (See Appendix). The Pas de Calais, at the narrowest part of the English Channel, was the most logical area for the assault and so became the focal point of most of the fabrications of the Allied plan.

The Germans had long thought that any possible Allied invasion would be an amphibious assault near Calais, so *Fortitude* merely confirmed what they had already assumed. They accepted the entire premise of the main Allied offensive being made there with almost no questions asked. The Germans fell so hard for the lies of *Fortitude* that it would be weeks after the Allied landings that they were finally convinced that the action taking place in Normandy was the actual invasion and not a diversion.

Operating under the assumption that the Allies were headed for the Pas de Calais they had, even before *Fortitude* was activated, constructed their strongest defenses and stationed the majority of their best troops there. Within 60 miles of Calais they had positioned five "static" (defensive) divisions, three first rate divisions, one reserve division, one Luftwaffen-Feld division and two armored divisions. Normandy on the other hand was covered by three static divisions, one first rate division, one Luftwaffen-Feld division and two armored divisions.

By the time they figured out that the Pas de Calais was not threatened and began moving reinforcements from the Calais area to Normandy, it was far too late to have any significant effect on the battle for the beaches. Even after they had realized the significance of the Normandy landings, the German high command insisted on leaving the majority of their best troops in their original positions near Calais. Unfortunately for them, they would still be sitting there when the Allies forces broke out of Normandy, all but cutting them off from Germany. Many did eventually escape across the Scheldt Estuary in Holland, but they would play almost no part in the defense of France.

An example of just how convinced the German High Command, (meaning Hitler), was that the Allies were eventually going to cross the Dover Straits for their main effort, is a directive issued by Hitler on July 8th. In it, he stated that the Allies could be expected to attempt to secure a seaport either on the French coast of the Mediterranean or on the Brittany Peninsula. The part of the edict that pertains even more directly to our story proclaims that a major invasion would occur in the Pas de Calais area that was defended by the German Fifteenth Army.

He also ordered that under no circumstances would it be allowable for forces from that unit be used to combat the "diversion" in Normandy.

Another reason that *Fortitude* was so much more successful than the Allies could have possibly hoped was the complete failure of the Germans to realize the magnitude of the immense logistical support required to stage an operation the size of the landings in Normandy. The Allies had committed all their resources to the invasion in Normandy. To have assumed that they could have launched a mere diversion the size of those landings and still had enough left to make a "main" landing at the Pas de Calais really reflects the German lack of experience in major amphibious operations and the logistics needed to support them.

Once they realized the extent of the operation, they needed to move to defeat it. Instead, they decided to merely contain it while they waited for the other shoe to fall in the form of the "real" invasion at Calais. If they had understood the immense requirements of an amphibious invasion, they, in all likelihood, would not have hesitated to do their utmost to eliminate the incursion in Normandy. Instead, they persisted in believing the fabrications of *Fortitude*. This in conjunction with their ignorance of amphibious operations would be the key to Allied success in the liberation of France.

That ignorance stemmed from an almost complete lack of experience in the amphibious field. The Germans had conducted relatively minor landings in the fjords of Norway in 1940, but the vast majority of their war had not required such planning. Again in 1940, when they were contemplating an invasion of Britain in what they called "*Operation Sea Lion*", their planning seemed to reflect the idea that it was merely a river crossing, a very large river granted, but a river all the same. Their almost comical collection of ferries, river barges and tug boats that were to be used in the assault was a clear indication of their total lack of comprehension when it came to the difficulties and the requirements of conducting a major amphibious operation.

Even if the Germans had appreciated the logistics involved, they had no way to confirm or deny the size and locations of the Allied stockpiles of men and supplies. Most of the agents they had managed to insert into Britain had been apprehended and turned by the British intelligence services or else they had been eliminated. These "double-agents" were then used to send information back to their handlers that confirmed many aspects of the *Fortitude* program.

The aerial reconnaissance forces available to the German commanders in France were all but nonexistent. In common with other branches of the German Air Force in France, the majority of their aircraft had either been destroyed or transferred to other theaters. The few German reconnaissance aircraft that managed to reach Britain were to a certain extent controlled by the Allies. The Allied control of the air over Britain was so complete that they could almost select which of them would survive to return to France. In this way, they could in some cases determine what locations were observed and what intelligence was returned to German headquarters.

When the initial planning for *Overlord* began, the Americans had actually been in favor of an attack against the Pas de Calais for many of the same reasons that the Germans considered it the most likely invasion site. It was not only the shortest transit distance from Britain, but also closer to Nazi Germany and thus, in American eyes, the fastest way to end the war. The British had cast their vote in favor of Normandy for a variety of very sound reasons; fortunately, the senior partners in the Allied alliance won this election.

One interesting aspect of the German decision to favor the Pas de Calais over other locations for the upcoming invasion was a surprising failure of their normally very efficient General Staff to consider the necessities for a successful Allied attack. Other than providing the shortest distance for the invasion forces to travel from Britain to the shores of France, the benefits of the Pas de Calais were far outweighed by its shortcomings. Even dispensing with the benefit of hindsight it is difficult to understand how the German High Command could not see the downside of Calais as an invasion point.

It was only 20 miles from Britain to the French coast at that point, but that narrow stretch acted as a funnel for the radical tidal conditions that prevail in the English Channel. It was also totally exposed to the wind which added considerably to the rougher seas that were to be encountered off-shore.

Those 20 miles would also have made it possible for the German defenders to observe Allied naval movements during their entire transit to the invasion beaches. There could be no surprise landings. The distance was so short that earlier in the war German long-range artillery had actually bombarded the port of Dover from their positions in France. The possibility of making the entire crossing while under intense shell-fire would have been daunting to even the most courageous sailor.

Even if the Allied target had been the Pas de Calais, the trip for the assault forces would not have been a voyage of a mere 20 miles. They would be leaving from ports a far away as Bristol on the Irish Sea, no matter what their final destination. There was no possible way they could all depart from the port of Dover where the eyes of the Germans were focused. Again, the German lack of maritime logistical understanding would cost them.

The Norman coast, in contrast to that of the Pas de Calais, offered somewhat better protection from the elements. On either end of the area designated for the assault, were formidable land masses. To the east was the point on which Le Havre was located and to the west was the Contentin Peninsula. This provided more protection from the prevailing wind patterns that are prevalent during the summer months than would the more exposed area off the Pas de Calais.

During the trip to Normandy the sea conditions encountered were manageable for the larger vessels responsible for transporting the smaller landing craft. The larger-sized landing craft which had to make the crossing under their own power had a harder time, but they survived. Many of their occupants were so sea-sick by the time they reached Normandy that they weren't sure that they would.

Although it was to be a 100-mile trip from the nearest point in Britain, across open waters to reach those calmer seas off Normandy, that would not be the most critical point of the invasion. That would occur when the smaller landing craft began moving from the transports to the shore once their destination had been reached. For them to safely reach that destination, they would need the calmest waters possible.

Even the somewhat safer seas off Normandy could become dangerous. At their worst, they could become violent enough to prompt postponement of the landings, as would indeed happen on the 5th of June. This situation could have been far worse had the target been the exposed beaches of Calais.

On the actual morning of D-Day, the wind came from the northwest, which was the wind direction expected for that time of the year. The assault forces on "Utah", to the leeward side of the Contentin Peninsula, had almost no surf to contend with while those on "Omaha" and the British beaches landed in waves approaching 4 feet in height. Even those 4-foot seas were preferable to what they would have encountered off the Pas de Calais.

Now for the matter of the physical distance from the French coast to Germany. Pas de Calais was obviously closer to the Nazi homeland than Normandy, but Germany was a future objective for the Allies. The more immediate goal of the invaders would be to securely establish themselves ashore. Operations which were destined for the future were of secondary concern. If they weren't on French soil, the distance to the German border would be the least of their problems.

Once they had established a foothold on the Continent though, they could adjust their operational planning to fit the situation. Even if Normandy had been a diversion as the Germans thought, if it had been successful, the Allies could have theoretically diverted forces there and made it their main effort. This was the issue that the Germans needed to focus upon. Their immediate concern should have been preventing of the Allies from establishing a secure beach-head anywhere, even if it wasn't in the most strategically sound location. But, they chose to become entranced with their maps and the few inches on those maps that separated Germany from the English Channel.

Instead of assuming the Allies would conduct themselves as expected, the German High Command should have given more thought to viable alternative possibilities. Unlike the Germans, whose experience in amphibious landings was nearly nonexistent, the Allies could be considered the World's experts in the field. Those amphibious experts had concluded early in their planning that the location that provided the best chance for a successful invasion was Normandy, not the more obvious choice of the Pas de Calais.

And then to the matter of the assault beaches themselves. The majority of the beaches in the Calais area weren't considered to be suitable for the landing of large number of troops and their supplies while under fire. They are, for the most part, small and are often overlooked by imposing and easily defended bluffs or even cliffs. The existence of similar geography at Dieppe in 1942 and at Normandy's bloody "*Omaha Beach*" in 1944 gives a fine example of what might have occurred if the Allies had chosen to land on the confined beaches that dominated the narrowest part of the English Channel.

If the Germans had recalled their victory over the Allied force which had attacked the Channel port of Dieppe in August of 1942, they might have looked at potential assault beaches differently. In the case of Dieppe, the port itself was heavily defended and the beach is flanked by two high bluffs which had enabled the German defenders to fire down and along the beach. They had all but wiped out the Canadian troops who were trapped like fish in a bowl. To have not acknowledged that the Allies might have learned from their costly mistake was a combination of ignorance and arrogance which would cost the Germans dearly.

Another requirement that the Allies had for the assault beaches were that they needed to be adjacent to one another. As soon as possible after the initial landings the individual beaches had to be joined into one. This would present a united front to the inevitable German counter-attacks that would follow once the German High Command realized the situation.

There were still other issues that worked against choosing the Pas de Calais as the site for the invasion. Even if the Allied Armies managed to get off those confined beaches, they had still more difficulties to deal with. One of those was the lay of the land once they had advanced from the shores of the English Channel. It was less than ideal for the construction of tactical airfields. This was an extremely important consideration for Allied planners. It must be remembered that the range of fighter aircraft was severely limited in the days of World War II, and so the closer to the frontlines they could be located the better. The vital need for immediate and close air support for the invading forces had been a powerful influence in the choice of possible invasion points for the Allies, even in the earliest stages of their planning. It had helped eliminate all but Normandy as a potential invasion target.

The conveniently flat and open areas around the city of Caen in Normandy, on the other hand were considered to be perfect for the construction of the needed airfields. The terrain also favored the maneuvering of large formations of armored vehicles. This was to be all-important in any attempt to break out of the beach-head, and to begin the march towards Germany.

The planners had felt that the occupation of Caen and the surrounding area was so vital to the success of *Overlord* that they had listed it as the No.1 priority for the invasion forces on D-Day. Unfortunately, for a variety of reasons, the city and its potential airfield sites were not secured by British and Canadian forces until almost a month after the invasion.

Another mark against picking the Pas de Calais as a possible assault point was size of the local seaports. As has been stated at various points in this text, the securing of cargo unloading facilities was elemental to the survival of the Allied forces. The Calais area harbors of Boulogne, Calais and Dunkirk had much smaller unloading capacities and were considered inadequate for the job of supporting major operations. The ports of Le Havre and Cherbourg in Normandy were judged to be more along the lines of what the Allies were looking for.

Although Cherbourg had been mainly a passenger terminus prior to the war, it was hoped that it would suffice as a cargo port until the capture of the larger Le Havre, which was the second largest French harbor after Marseilles on the southern coast. In addition, it was hoped that the ports along the Brittany coast to the south would also be taken and could be used to supplement the supply chain until larger facilities could be secured.

These smaller ports would hopefully enable the Allied beachhead to survive the first critical days after the landings. The differing potential of those, hopefully soon to be under Allied control, supply points was given the highest consideration when choosing the invasion site. Ports of lesser size would naturally disperse the limited supplies that could be landed and would initially confuse the system for moving them to the front. The perfect situation would have been to use one or two larger locations as primary destinations for the supplies and personnel required by the Allied Expeditionary Force. But, until that occurred, a series of the largest harbors available would have to do.

Hitler's staff officers had long assured him that if Germany held the ports, Germany held the continent. Without a reliable source of supplies, any attempt by the Allies to invade was doomed. They could land, but they couldn't survive. Hitler agreed and proceeded to declare the Channel and Brittany seaports "fortresses". They were never to be surrendered. The garrisons were to fight to the last man and to make sure the ports were destroyed if they were in danger of being lost. From past experience Hitler's commanders knew better than to disobey a *"Fuhrer Directive"* and they wouldn't do so this time either. In the main, the plan worked as well as could be reasonably expected. The spirited defense and destruction of the Brittany ports, as well as that at Le Havre complicated the supply situation for the Allies and forced them to adapt their plans.

The Allies had originally planned to occupy the ports of Brest, L'orient and St.Nazaire along the Brittany coast to help supply their forces on the southern flank. But, as so often happens in war, plans changed. In following Hitler's orders, the German defenders would prove to be much more tenacious and destructive than hoped for b the Allied planners. The port of Brest wasn't taken until September 24th, more than three months after the invasion. When the Americans finally entered Brest, they found that the German garrison had done such a thorough job of destruction that the port and its facilities would be of no use to them until early the next year. By that time, it could help in the reconstruction of post-war France, but would serve no useful purpose in the actual war effort.

The garrisons in the ports of Dunkirk, L'Orient, St. Nazaire, and La Rochelle along the Channel and Biscay coasts would also follow orders. They would hold out until the end of the war. The Allies could have taken any or all of these ports whenever they wanted, but they realized that by the time they had taken and restored them, the harbors would be so far to the rear of the frontlines as to be nearly useless for supporting combat operations. This, along with the needless casualties they would have to endure, convinced the Allied high command that a battle for the Channel ports was a battle they didn't need to fight.

The decision was made by the Allied High Command to contain these diehards in their self-imposed confinement with the use of the minimum force necessary and get on with winning the war. These isolated pockets of German resistance did end up serving a purpose for the Allies. In order to contain the German garrisons, many Allied units new to the Theater were posted around the port perimeters. In this way, they could be exposed to potential action without the severe consequences that could be encountered on the frontlines.

Later, in the month of September, the taking of the ports of Dieppe (taken on the 1st but not operational until the 8th), Dunkirk (held out until the end of the war) Boulogne (taken in October) and Calais (taken in November) along the Channel coast was assigned to the Canadian Army. They were eventually secured, but by that time, the need for small ports had all but passed. What was required now was a large; no, make that a huge seaport. That was to be the harbor was at Antwerp in Belgium. It was destined to eventually become the main supply point for both the American and British Allied Army Groups, not just the British as had been the original plan.

But, due to poor planning on the part of the British 21st Army Group and various distractions (i.e. *Operation Market/Garden*) suffered by Field Marshal Montgomery, the British commander, Antwerp was not to be available as had been hoped. This delay allowed the bulk of the German 15th Army to escape from the trap at Pas de Calais. They were then able to flee over the Scheldt Estuary to the west of Antwerp and back safely to German-held territory.

All along, the Allies knew that when they finally did manage to capture a major harbor, it would be a long time before they could make use of it. The Germans were masters at disabling seaports, as well as the infrastructures so vital to their operations. In earlier operations in the Mediterranean Theater, whenever the Allies took possession of a harbor they could count on weeks, if not months, of delay until it was fully operational again. They would learn the truth of this when they eventually took Cherbourg.

The Allied invasion plan called for Cherbourg, which was the port nearest to the invasion beaches, to be taken on D+17. That meant a minimum of two weeks before they had the faintest hope of having an actual seaport in which they could unload the bulk of their heavier supplies. And even when they did take it, the odds that the Germans would be willing to leave it as a functioning entity that could be used immediately were slim indeed.

According to "the Book", which was the nickname for the very secret and very detailed plan for *Operation Neptune-Overlord* and its immediate aftermath, the best-case scenario would have had Cherbourg operating as a viable port on D+47. This meant if the Allies were extremely lucky, they would only have about 9 weeks of lugging all their supplies across open beaches. Those beaches would be totally exposed to the vagaries of the less than stable weather patterns which have ruled the English Channel since its creation. Even if everything went as scheduled, something which seldom happens in war, the invading forces would be without a reliable supply base during the most vulnerable time in the existence of the beach-head.

They couldn't count on the Germans continuing to believe the fabrications of *Operation Fortitude* and keeping the majority of their forces in the wrong place. The Germans would be coming and the Allied troops would desperately need the means to stop them.

There was only one other option to taking Cherbourg that might have been considered. That would have been the larger port of Le Havre, which was located well to the east of the invasion area. But it would have suffered the same depredations by the Germans as the nearby Cherbourg, and so nothing would have been gained by choosing it. In the event, that port wasn't taken until the September 12th, by which date the harbor as well as the city had been all but destroyed by the combined efforts of the Royal Air Force's Bomber Command and the German garrison. It wasn't reopened for shipping until October 7th.

Le Havre had also never been given serious consideration as a target for the landings because of its proximity to the River Seine. Due to the location of the suitable beaches in the area it would have been necessary to split the assault forces on either side of the river. This situation would have exposed the Allied invasion force to possible defeat in detail. If one portion was attacked, it could expect no immediate assistance from its sister units across the river.

The Allies realized that time was of the essence because the Germans would not fail to mount a counter-offensive as soon as they realized that Normandy was the location of the actual invasion. The Allies would need a secure beach-head as well as a steady flow of supplies to withstand the expected German assault. They had to have a reliable supply base they could count on to support the frontline soldiers when the inevitable attack came. Not one that was totally dependent on good weather, as the open beaches were.

Throughout the war, the German Wehrmacht had acquired a reputation for immediately counter-attacking to regain lost territory. It had been ingrained into the German soldier that the best chance you had to defeat your enemy was strike back before he had a chance to consolidate his gains and improve his defenses. That philosophy applied whether it was a single soldier or an entire army, and there was no reason to expect them to change.

When the Allies finally got down to the serious business of planning an invasion, most of these details and issues still lay well in the future. Many would have to be dealt with as they arose. One which was appreciated beforehand and could be considered in the initial planning was that of logistics.

There are several well-known authors that have expressed the opinion that the Allied planners of *Overlord* over-emphasized the need for port facilities in the initial assault phase of the attack on German-held Europe. They apparently felt that logistical concerns were placed too high on the list of requirements for a successful invasion. This line of thought is hard to understand when one looks at the supply issues that were to plague the Allied armies every step of the way from the beaches of Normandy to the banks of the Elbe River in Germany at the end of the war. The longer the Allies went without a proper seaport, the larger the supply deficit they would eventually have to overcome.

Without a harbor of some sort at the earliest moment there was no possibility of landing enough supplies to enable the Allied armies on the Continent to survive. The Allies needed the facilities to efficiently unload their supplies in order to be victorious. That was as true at the very beginning of the campaign as much as it was at the end.

Everyone involved realized that something out of the ordinary was needed. What they came up with was to be extraordinary indeed.

MULBERRY-A SOLUTION?

At the *Quebec Conference* (codenamed "*Quadrant*") which took place in August of 1943, one the main objectives was to approve a final plan for the invasion of northwestern France. In this meeting between the British and the Americans, there were many critical decisions to be made on a variety of global strategic questions, but the one that concerns this book is the approval of the plan for that long-awaited attack.

In an interesting sidelight, which actually has nothing to do with our story but is interesting none the less, is that it had been decided to exclude the Canadians from any participation in the gathering. It does seem a bit odd in that the conference was held on Canadian soil and that when the invasion actually occurred the Canadians would supply approximately one-fifth of the assault troops. It didn't really pay to be a junior partner when the big boys were discussing strategy.

Of those in attendance almost everyone had an idea or an opinion that they felt would ensure success for this "one shot deal" that the Allies were finally going to commit to. It was generally acknowledged by all the participants that if this invasion failed, there in all likelihood would not be another attempt.

One of the many proposals that the British brought with them concerning the invasion involved the novel idea of a prefabricated harbor. Until this time, the idea of a transportable harbor had existed mainly in the realm of a few rather eccentric dreamers.

When the British representatives began their discussions with the Americans about what eventually became *Mulberry*, they had a concept and nothing else. No design, not even a solid majority of favorable opinions on the part of their own planning staff concerning the actual feasibility of such a project. What they did have was a rather farfetched solution to an issue that had been hanging over any Allied return to France. The troops could be landed, but they had to have sufficient supplies to survive. If they didn't have the ammunition and fuel to fight with, they might as well stay in Britain.

In war risks have to be taken, but if some of those risks can be eliminated or reduced then so much the better. In an endeavor as dangerous and unique as *Overlord*, there was more than the usual amount of potential disasters to deal with. Any and all possible solutions to any questions had to be considered, no matter how seemingly bizarre. At any other time, an idea as radical as *Mulberry* would not have even been considered by serious-minded military professionals. But this was not a normal military operation and even less than conventional solutions couldn't be ignored.

Even with that mindset, the Americans weren't really impressed with the prospects of what they in large part considered just another hare-brained British scheme. And they weren't the least bit shy in voicing their concerns and doubts. In the end though, the British would carry the day with their arguments. This they seemed to do at most of the inter-Allied conferences, unless the Soviet Premier Joseph Stalin was involved.

When Stalin was seated at the table the odds were that he was not going to be affected by opinions or emotions, or even facts. He could afford to be hard-nosed and uncompromising. His country was facing the bulk of the German Army and everyone, including British Prime Minister Churchill knew it. If he decided to take his chips and leave the table, the western Allies were all but doomed. When Stalin talked, Churchill and Roosevelt listened. But, if "Uncle Joe" Stalin was absent from the negotiations the British generally had a much easier time of it.

The success of the British at the various conferences had much to do with preparation and organization. The American military leaders were basically rookies when it came to dealing with allies. The British had much more experience with joint operations. They had negotiating with allies for centuries.

Their staff work often seemed to the Americans to be overly complicated and ponderous, but when they sat down at the conference table, they had all the facts and counter-arguments at hand. It also didn't hurt that more often than not; Prime Minister Churchill could sway President Roosevelt to his way of thinking.

Prior to the conference in Quebec, there had been many on the British side that were less than thrilled the idea of transporting and assembling an entire seaport off the hostile coast of France. Two of the senior skeptics are especially noteworthy. They were Vice Admiral Bertram Ramsay, who would eventually be named as overall Commander of *Neptune*, the naval assault portion of Overlord, and Rear Admiral William G. Tennant, who would actually be in command of the entire *Mulberry* operation itself. It is interesting that men in such positions of authority directly related to *Mulberry* would have serious doubts about its use or practicality.

During the trip over to North America for the conference, British Lord Louis Mountbatten, Commander of Combined Operations, had invited several of these less than convinced staff officers into one of his staterooms aboard the RMS QUEEN MARY. When they entered, they found a partially filled bathtub, approximately 40 paper boats and a Mae West life vest. Professor J.D. Bernal, one of Mountbatten's senior scientific advisors, was in charge of the demonstration. One of those at this somewhat unique get together was the First Sea Lord, Admiral Sir Dudley Pound. Pound chose to stand on a toilet so that he could better view the proceedings.

On the command of "More waves please, Lieutenant Grant", Lieutenant Commander D.A. Grant apparently being the lowest ranking member in attendance and the only one with the required scrub brush (a handy wave-maker) began the display. A group of the paper boats were placed in the open waters of the tub. They were soon swamped by the Grant-induced waves. Another paper flotilla was then positioned within the protective confines of the Mae West. It naturally fared much better than its predecessor and hopefully exhibited the possibilities of a portable harbor.

Even if this rather elementary demonstration didn't convince all the attendees, it hopefully got them thinking along the right lines. Even if it hadn't, the British were determined to show a united front in their negotiations with the Americans, no matter their personal views on the project.

Who actually came up with the concept of a moveable harbor is not known for certain. More than 60 years after the event, all of the major participants are gone and the few publications to be found on the subject often give conflicting stories about the origin of the idea. In all likelihood it was a team effort with many people contributing a thought, a question or even an argument to the Genesis of *Mulberry*.

But an idea has to originate somewhere and there are a few serious contenders for the title of originator of what came to be known as *Mulberry*. It would seem that Royal Navy Commodore John Hughes-Hallett, Welsh designer Hugh Iorys Hughes, Professor J.D. Bernal and Winston Churchill would be the leading candidates.

Hughes-Hallett had previously served as the naval commander for the ill-fated Dieppe raid in 1942. He was later appointed as Naval Chief of Staff to the planners of *Neptune-Overlord*. The story on Hughes-Hallett was that while attending an early meeting concerning the invasion of France, he, half in jest, suggested that if the Allies couldn't capture a functioning seaport maybe they should take one with them. After the laughter had died down, a more serious discussion took place about what might be actually be involved in such an operation.

The initial idea was simply for a breakwater to be constructed of obsolete ships. They would be scuttled just off-shore, providing a temporary barrier against the action of the waves that could disrupt the beaching of landing craft on the assault beaches. These small craft were extremely vulnerable to even moderate surf conditions and thus needed all the assistance they could get.

Another participant at the same meeting, British Army Major General C.N. Browning, suggested that equal thought should be given to some sort of equipment to assist in the unloading of the larger ships. Somewhere along the line, the breakwater idea was abandoned or forgotten. All efforts were then focused on developing a stand-alone type of system which would allow cargo and troops to be moved directly from the ships off-shore onto the beach. The necessity of the discarded breakwater scheme would become much more evident at a later date.

The next potential originator of the idea was Welsh inventor and designer Hugh Iorys Hughes. In this version, Hughes had been working with the idea of some sort of off-shore unloading system since the Allied evacuation at Dunkirk in 1940. By June of 1942, he was spending most of his time and energy on a possible design. He later mentioned his progress with the idea to his brother-in-law, who happened to be a co-worker of Commodore Hughes-Hallett. Reportedly, the brother-in-law then passed on the idea to the Commodore who then brought it up at the aforementioned meeting.

The next contender, Professor Bernal, was the primary scientific advisor to the commander of British Combined Operations, Lord Louis Mountbatten. Supposedly when inquiries were made as to the possibility of some type off-shore apparatus to assist in the unloading of invasion shipping, he had already been contemplating such a problem. He had already begun developing ideas concerning the design. Bernal would be heavily involved in the later design and construction phases of the various components of *Mulberry*. Whether this was due to his being the originator of the idea or merely to the position he held in Mountbatten's organization is difficult to determine.

On May 30, 1942 Winston Churchill had sent a memorandum to Mountbatten concerning the feasibility of a floating pier off an invasion beach as opposed to a fixed trestle type. Churchill was known to have a predilection for odd ideas or inventions. Many of them were truly bizarre. One of the most memorable was an aircraft carrier that was to be constructed of ice. As with many of Churchill's schemes, wiser heads had prevailed and that plan too was soon discarded for a variety of practical reasons.

But the odds were with him, and in this instance his proposal actually had some merit. With the 20+ foot tidal fluctuations in the English Channel, a fixed structure could be at water level and functioning at low tide and submerged and totally useless at high tide. A floating unit was indeed the most viable solution.

During the First World War Churchill, as First Lord of the Admiralty, had proposed facilitating the capture of the German-held islands of Borkum and Sylt by using a breakwater. It was to consist of several flat-bottomed barges which would be scuttled off-shore. The idea was to provide the calmer waters which were needed for landing troops and supplies on the otherwise unprotected beaches. The plan had never been realized, but Churchill had no doubt stored the idea away for future reference. So, even the British Prime Minister could make a claim to being the person responsible for planting the seed of the *Mulberry*.

With all these possible candidates, the theory of invention by committee seems the most likely hypothesis. In any case, whoever was responsible for any part of one of the most creative and interesting engineering concepts in military history deserves to be remembered along with their project.

After the approval of the *Mulberry* project by Churchill, Roosevelt and the Combined Chiefs of Staff at Quebec, the allocation of construction responsibilities for the various components had to be delegated out. At a further meeting on September 3, 1943, it was decided that the majority of the work would go to the British.

In spite of Britain's already over-extended industrial base, the construction of Mulberry in the U.S. was never seriously considered. America could have handled the entire complex program with no strain, but it was only 7 months before the anticipated date of the invasion. The transporting of the completed harbor components across the stormy Atlantic would have taken much too long and been far too dangerous. *Mulberry* would have serious issues just crossing the English Channel. It would have been courting disaster to have attempted towing them across the North Atlantic.

There was also the fact that the American military would have been less than ecstatic about being force fed what in their eyes was just another British gimmick. In their opinion, there were much better uses for the industrial might of America. The Americans had their own plans for winning the war, and they didn't include constructing a farfetched

British design which might or might not work. Let the British spend their own time and money building what was considered by many senior American officers to be a waste of both. At the very least, it was considered a distraction from the main effort of the invasion.

If they had been given a vote on the matter, the majority of US military leaders would have taken a pass on the entire project, not just the construction phase. In the end though, the man in the White House approved of the idea. That meant that even raging Anglophobes like US Navy Commander-in-Chief Admiral Ernest J. King had to bite their tongues and go along with the idea.

As soon as the British Admiralty and War Office received the go-ahead from Quebec, they immediately began making preparations for the construction of the *Mulberry* components. It was soon decided that nearly 20,000 men would need to be assigned to the work force.

Before the project was finally completed, there would be several hundred different sub-contracting businesses involved, as well as a labor force of over 45,000. Unfortunately, many of those 45,000 were unskilled laborers that had to be trained on the job. This would lead to many delays, as well as various building flaws in the *Mulberry* units themselves.

But, before any construction could begin, a design had to be chosen. It was decided that there were three designs that would compete for the floating roadway contract, which at this time was the only portion of *Mulberry* that was being considered. The breakwater project would be added at a later date after testing sessions had emphasized the need for it.

The first contestant for the contract was a system of concrete "*Hippo*" pier-heads which were capable of being towed to France. They looked much like massive bridge piers topped with steel structures that rose above the surface of the water. Atop that framework would be attached tubular steel "*Crocodile*" bridge units which would connect them to one another and to the shore. The design wasn't really the floating roadway/pier that had been visualized in the initial concept. It was more of a fixed structure that could be towed and then set on the ocean floor. This was the brainchild of inventor Hugh Iorys Hughes.

Hippo and Crocodile pier system

The Hughes's pier-heads would serve an unexpected purpose later in the program, when minus their superstructures, they would be used as preliminary models for what became the "*Phoenix*" caissons in the *Mulberry* breakwater system.

As there were no available dry-docks of sufficient size in which to construct the Hughes prototypes, it was decided to build them on a golf course at Conwy in North Wales. Due to space limitations it was necessary to launch the 3,200-ton piers sideways into a river. They would be the largest vessels launched in this manner up to this time. They would then be towed up the coast to the testing area on the west coast of Scotland.

The British Admiralty itself put forward a design created by inventor Ronald Hamilton. A physical disability had prevented Hamilton from serving in the military so he had occupied much of his time designing flexible floating units in the hope that the requirement for such a device might arise in the future.

His invention was to be known as the "*Swiss Roll*", due to its appearance when stored. Its main advantages were economy and simplicity. It consisted of timber and canvas secured by steel cables and was simply rolled out across the water. Theoretically surface tension and the short side boards provided would keep it and its load afloat. It was an interesting concept, but one which was probably not considered a serious contender in the competition due to its extremely fragile construction.

A Swiss Roll roadway

The third proposal was submitted by the Transportation5 (Tn5) department of the Army's War Office. It consisted of a series of flexible bridge units that were to be connected to one another. They would then be attached to floating steel pontoons which supported them on the surface of the water. The original designer of the bridge units was Lieutenant Colonel William T. Everall.

Everall had earned the bulk of his reputation building bridges in pre-war India. After the fall of France in 1940, the War Office had asked him to design a flexible ramp to facilitate the movement of locomotives off Channel steamers. It was anticipated that there would be a shortage of rolling rail stock in France when they made their eventual return to the Continent, and so they would have to take their own.

Although Everall was designing what he thought was to be basically an off-loading ramp for shipping, he must be given credit for doing the early concept work for what eventually became the *"Whale"* floating roadway. In early 1943, Everall received orders sending him to Washington D.C. He was then ably replaced by his assistant, Major Allan Beckett of the Royal Engineers.

Beckett would finish the design for the unloading ramp, while adding many of his own refinements to it. When the need for a floating roadway arose, he simply modified the ramp and added floating pontoons, which he also designed.

In the end, he would receive the lion's share of the somewhat limited acclaim for the project. After the war, Beckett would be one of the few key figures in *Operation Mulberry* to garner any sort of recognition or reward for their part in it. In 1949, he was appointed a Member of the British Empire (Military) and awarded 3,000 English pounds for his contributions to the success of D-Day. He would use the money to buy a house in Farnborough, Kent where he lived until his death on June 19, 2005, at the age of 91.

The site chosen for the testing of the three designs was an area near the fishing village of Garlieston on the Scottish side of the Solway Firth. The beaches and tidal conditions were found to be similar to those off of Normandy. It was there that the three contestants would be subjected to various conditions while operating under full loads.

During the testing, the Hughes design was found to suffer from an unexpected movement caused by the currents "scouring", or removing the sand by the tides from underneath the massive *Hippo* piers. This caused the piers to shift their positions. The *Crocodile* roadways which rested on them then became severely distorted and nearly useless. It soon became obvious that their fixed construction prevented them from being flexible enough to withstand the wild tidal fluctuations that had to be dealt with in the English Channel.

After the testing was completed, the *Hippo* test model was discarded and left in the mud of Rigg Bay, west of Garlieston in southwest Scotland. It could still be seen there until March of 2006 when it was destroyed in a storm.

Hamilton's *Swiss Roll* as expected, was found to be totally lacking in its load carrying capacity. When a standard-sized cargo truck was driven over the test unit, it sank beneath the surface. Modifications were made, but the maximum load the design would carry was 7 tons. That was far from the 38-ton (the weight of a tank) capacity required. The design was not completely discarded though. Several examples were utilized off Arromanches in Normandy for off-loading some lighter cargos, such as troops and small vehicles.

The winner of the competition was to be the War Office's Tn5 Department design for a flexible bridge roadway. Any doubt that the right choice had been made was removed when a storm rolled through the area soon after testing was completed. It severely damaged the losers and caused only minor damage to the victor.

After the proto-type bridge units had won the competition, it was decided that a system of anchoring their seaward ends to the sea bottom was needed. The adjustable pier-head design that was eventually chosen would serve two purposes. It would not only secure the roadways in position; it would provide a more spacious area for unloading cargo. We will have more on these very creative and important units later.

After the conclusion of the tests in Scotland, Prime Minister Winston Churchill invited one of the losing designers, Hugh Iorys Hughes, to become a consultant on the project. Churchill said the appointment was due to Hughes' early commitment to the idea of a prefabricated pier system, as well as his expertise in the field. Hughes would later assist in the construction of various components for *Mulberry*. He would also help to identify areas off Selsey and Dungeness that would be used to "park" the caisson breakwaters after their construction.

It had become obvious to the engineers involved in the testing that the previously discarded idea of a breakwater system was needed after all. All three of the competing designs had suffered from even moderate wave-action. Even the winning floating roadway system, which had survived the post-testing storm, was considered far too frail to withstand the continuous pounding that was sure to be encountered in the English Channel. Rear Admiral William Tennant, who would be in overall charge of the *Mulberries*, seconded the idea that there was a need for at least some sort of temporary protection while the harbors were under construction off Normandy. This proposal would eventually lead to the "*Gooseberry*" system of caissons and block-ships.

Admiral Tennant's previous experience in this war had included assisting in the organization of the Allied evacuation at Dunkirk in May of 1940. He had also been the Captain of the Royal Navy battle-cruiser REPULSE when she was sunk by Japanese aircraft off Malaya in December 1941. Since then he had served in a variety of staff assignments.

The testing program had revealed several other issues that had to be addressed. It had been found that it was extremely difficult for the construction crews to align the individual 480-foot bridge sections of the winning Tn5 design for assembly in even the mildest sea. After much experimenting, a remedy was discovered in the form of what were called "erection tanks". They were 16-feet long, 8-feet in diameter and barrel-shaped. They would be filled with compressed air and placed under the bridge sections. The movement and elevation of the units could then be controlled by adjusting the amount of compressed air in the tanks.

Erection tank

Another problem that the crews had to contend with was that of securely anchoring the long roadways to the sea bottom. Concrete blocks weighing 5 tons each were tried. They worked well enough, but the transporting and placement of these behemoths made the proposition totally unacceptable. Engineer Allan Beckett came to the rescue with his design for a *"Kite Anchor"* that was so effective that many of them that were used off Normandy could not be recovered from the seabed after the war. They were imbedded too deeply and so were just left in place. The only example known to still exist is on display at a museum in Vierville-sur-Mer.

Kite anchor

Even after a basic design had been chosen, other bits and pieces were continually added until the entire picture was complete. As would be expected, a project as complex as a portable seaport has an almost overwhelming list of components. To keep this book of a manageable size, we will concern ourselves with only the larger parts of the puzzle.

First of all is the name *Mulberry* itself. As is often the case with military code words, it holds no secret or implied meaning; it was merely the next approved code word on a list kept at the British War Office. But, in the case of some of the other code names in this story there were reasons for choosing them and those will be dealt with later.

The most recognizable part of a *Mulberry* harbor was to be the "*Phoenix*" caisson. It was an integral part of the breakwater system which protected the harbor facilities closer inshore. Initially there were to have been 147 built, but at a later stage in the planning for *Operation Neptune-Overlord*, it was decided that the projected life of the *Mulberries* would be extended. The previously planned decommissioning month of September was changed to at least December. This would require a "winterization" program of adding another line of caissons to backup or reinforce the older units against the heavy winter seas of the Channel. Construction would thus have to continue throughout the summer and would eventually total 212 caissons.

The fact that most of the surviving caissons that can still be seen off Arromanches in Normandy are later editions is a good indication of the different standards to which they were built. After the passing of the D-Day deadline, more time and care could be taken in the construction, and improvements could be made in the design itself.

The structures themselves were huge, basically hollow, concrete blocks. The interiors were divided into numerous compartments that were equipped with a series of valves to facilitate their flooding. They varied in size from the A1 model which was 204 feet long and weighed in at 6,044 tons to the D1 which stretched to 174 feet, but weighed only 1,672 tons. The reason for the size differential was that the bigger units could be placed in deeper water, while the smaller ones would be positioned closer to the shore in shallower waters. When placed in the proper position, they would stand 30 feet above the surface of the sea at low tide and 10 feet at high tide.

In the scramble to complete the project on schedule, the planners had overlooked a seemingly obvious and simple issue. When the time came to actually store the finished units, no one accepted responsibility for securing them in their assigned areas. The Army said their job was finished after they had completed the caissons and delivered them to the Navy. The Admiralty was of the opinion that delivery wasn't complete until the caissons were anchored in their final positions off Normandy. They further stated that even if it was decided that it was their responsibility to moor the caissons, they didn't have enough anchors or chains to do the job properly.

This problem would never have arisen but for the bickering and the territorial jealousies that existed between the two services. It had led to an almost complete communication breakdown between the Army and the Navy concerning the *Mulberry* project. If there had been a unified staff in overall control of the entire operation, this minor detail would have been taken care of during the preliminary planning stages.

This was not the first, nor would it be the last occasion when the almost juvenile actions by senior commanders on both sides of the war would have a detrimental effect on an operation. All too often during the war, leaders both civilian and military, would forget the "big picture" and personal agendas would take priority over the greater good. Fortunately, in this instance for the Allies, lives weren't lost, only time and the patience of many of those involved.

This situation has been all too common throughout military history. Petty insecurities concerning what could be termed territorial rights have often come to the forefront. The case of *Mulberry* would prove no different. Inter-service rivalries had begun clouding the *Mulberry* issue almost from its conception. Considering that it was a project that few were initially enthusiastic about in the beginning, it is interesting that everyone involved now wanted to be in control.

The Royal Navy's Admiralty and the Army's War Office had immediately begun squabbling over everything from construction responsibilities to the actual layout of the ports off the invasion beaches. These disputes would eventually lead to an almost complete lack of communication between the two services on the project. The consequence of this would be that some aspects, such as the storage of the completed units, of the program would be duplicated or compromised, while others were ignored or overlooked.

Several meetings between the two services were held concerning the problem, but nothing had been resolved. Finally, on December 15, 1943, at a conference chaired by the Chief of Staff to the Supreme Allied Commander, British General Frederick Morgan, it was decided that the Army would be in charge of designing and constructing the concrete caissons. They would also be responsible their scuttling off the invasion beach. The Navy would have the job of delivering the components across the Channel. They would also devise the actual layout of the harbor and would be in command of the harbor's operation after its completion. The "agreement" proved to be as dysfunctional as it appears.

It was vainly hoped by all involved that this meeting had settled all the issues concerning *Mulberry* that existed between the two organizations. Unfortunately, that was not to be the case, for whatever reason the British had decided that a joint headquarters for the project wasn't needed. The split command structure that resulted would continue to cause problems for the British and their *"Mulberry B"* until it was dismantled in December.

The codename *"Phoenix"* was eventually chosen for the caissons when it was decided, after much debate, that upon completion, each unit would be towed to a "parking area". It would then be intentionally sunk in shallow water. When it was needed off Normandy it would be then be pumped out with a yet to be determined exterior pumping system. It would then rise from its ashes, so to speak, just like the mythical bird.

The idea of intentionally sinking the caissons and raising them at a later date had never really arisen during the initial design and planning phases of *Mulberry*. Some accounts claim that part of the original design had called for compressed air tanks to be installed when the units were constructed, as far as can be ascertained this was not the case. It would probably have been discarded even if it had. Not only was there no need for it as the project had been originally conceived, it would have added considerably more expense. It would also have further complicated an already complex and difficult assignment for the construction crews.

A patchwork pumping system was eventually conceived for the recovery operation. The fact that the first *Phoenix* caisson wasn't even delivered until February 27th prevented any actual testing of the new and untried system until March 1944. Unfortunately, this session of testing didn't reveal all the problems that would arise during the operation. More on those later.

In another case of the incomplete planning that had been almost become a trademark of the project, it was soon found that there weren't any British tugs available to tow the first of the British-built *Phoenixes* to the testing area. It seemed that all the tugs of suitable capacity in the British Isles were already employed in other crucial service. The British were forced to swallow their pride and request the use of two US Navy tugs to do the job.

The parking areas chosen for the *Phoenixes* were located near Dungeness, Pagham and the Cant in southeastern Britain. These locations were chosen due to their proximity to Normandy, as well as the proper water depth and flat sea bottoms that would be required for the successful sinking and raising of the caissons.

Due to design flaws, poor construction techniques used by the unskilled labor force and deficient parking procedures there would often be unnecessary delays and losses when it came time to raise these 5-story high, city block-long, monsters from the bottom.

The lack of proper construction procedures showed itself early in the program. One of the first caissons laid down actually collapsed killing and injuring several of the crew that had been building it. Because of the schedule the crews were forced to work under, and the lack of experience of those crews, the quality of their work naturally suffered. Several caissons actually had to be destroyed when they developed severe cracks during the pouring of the thousands of tons of concrete required for their completion.

One of the many arguments against *Mulberry* had been the amount of construction materiel it would consume in an era of war-time shortages. The caissons did their share in justifying the complaints by using 330,000 cubic yards of reinforced concrete, 31,000 tons of steel and 1.5 million yards of steel shuttering. Before construction had commenced, agreements had been reached that the project would not have a serious detrimental effect on what were considered more vital programs. It was still a huge and, in many minds, highly questionable expenditure of resources.

The *Phoenix* caissons were constructed at several sites around the southern coast of Britain. One of the few remaining locations left to us is on Stansmore Point at Lepe on the Solent near Portsmouth. A construction crew of 700 men built six caissons this spot. The launching slipways can still be seen.

Phoenix construction

On their trip to Normandy, the caissons would be limited to a maximum speed of 5 miles per hour. This meant that if that speed limit was obeyed, the trip to France would take more than 30 hours. There would be many times during the 100-mile crossing that the tug boat crews responsible for getting them across the Channel would ignore that restriction. Admittedly, it was often for what seemed a good reason at the time, such as trying to stay ahead of bad weather or even the possibility of German surface craft in the area. But, whatever the excuse, it often led to damage to the fragile and poorly constructed *Phoenix*.

On their one and only sea voyage, the caissons were to be served by a crew of 6, two sailors and four soldiers who manned a Bofors anti-aircraft gun. That single gun was often their only protection from German attack.

There would be losses in transit, although not as many as might have been expected. One *Phoenix* was sunk by a German S-boat during the voyage. Another was lost to a mine and two more were lost due to bad weather. Another caisson broke its tow off Shoeburyness in Britain, ran aground and was badly damaged. It can still be seen there today. Another was a victim of poor parking procedures and broke apart when it settled to the bottom. It is still there resting in 40 feet of water off Pagham.

One aspect in the moving of the caissons and their numerous smaller cousins across the English Channel is often ignored by present-day historians, just as it was in early 1944 by the planners of *Mulberry*. Incredible as it may seem, the requirement for the tugboats needed to tow the harbors had seems to have been overlooked in the rush to complete the project. This "new" situation created a near panic on both sides of the Atlantic. Personnel were frantically sent to every possible location in a search of tugboats of almost any size or condition. In the rush that ensued, it was only to be expected that the quality of many of the vessels and crews acquired would be less than desired. This was yet another case in which a unified command structure for *Mulberry* might have eliminated an unnecessary and avoidable problem. There is the possibility that during preliminary planning the issue had been put on a back burner to be resolved later and then merely forgotten. But, whatever the reason, postponing a resolution to the question had merely shortened the available period in which to solve it. Now the date of the invasion was fast approaching and there weren't enough tugs to do the job.

The US Navy figured they had already fulfilled their tugboat obligations to *Mulberry* by allocating 25 completely unsuitable auxiliary minesweepers for the job. They didn't feel as though they could spare any actual tugs, so they sent minesweepers! These vessels were completely unsuitable for the task at hand. They were rated at 1,500 horsepower, which was powerful enough, but they were not equipped for any type of towing. The fact that their primary function would be exactly that seemed to have escaped the attention of the USN officers in charge. It was simply another case of the Americans doing no more than they felt was absolutely necessary to support a project that many of them considered a waste of time.

It was estimated that at least 200 ocean-going tugs would be needed to transport *Mulberry* to Normandy. The Allies would eventually have to make do with only 152 when D-Day finally arrived. It was not only the number of tugs that was an issue, but their size. In order to perform their functions properly, they had to be rated at least 750 h.p. Anything smaller could be used for auxiliary services, but could not be expected to tow any of the larger components across the open sea.

Tugs moving one of the smaller caissons

In the event, many of the tugs that were eventually used were supplied by the US Army Transportation Service (ATS). This may seem a bit odd, but a little-known fact is that the US Army had actually more commissioned vessels than did the US Navy during World War II. They were in the main transports and harbor craft, but there were a lot of them.

The main problem with the Army tugs was that many were manned by civilian crews. Those tended to be not as reliable or as dedicated as they needed to be for the dangerous job ahead. In many cases, their motivation could also be called into question. Although it would have been preferred that a spirit of adventure or even patriotism would be the incentive for their presence, many were more concerned with financial gain. Those potential malcontents were constantly reminding the military that they were civilians and as such weren't required to follow military regulations or commands. They were above that. Also, the contracts they had signed before leaving the United States for Europe had stated that they were to only participate in a non-combatant role. Unfortunately, the term "non-combatant" had never been clearly defined to those involved.

The problems that arose with many of the civilian crews while under peaceful conditions in Britain led to much speculation by the military authorities as to whether they would perform their jobs when they actually came under German fire. Would they leave their tows and return to Britain without authorization, or would they even complete their mission? The Army high command did not feel that it was in a position to summarily release and replace the potentially unreliable civilians, so the problem continued to fester. The issue was finally resolved, ironically by a German propaganda radio broadcast.

Germany's propaganda pawn "Lord Haw-Haw" proclaimed that German intelligence had ascertained the purpose of the collection of bizarre structures sitting off the south coast of Britain. He then proceeded to declare that the mighty Luftwaffe would blow them out of the water in the very near future.

In actuality they were mistaken in their assumptions about *Mulberry*. They had concluded that the main function of *Mulberry* was to provide mobile defensive anti-aircraft positions for the defense of captured harbors. In that they were wrong, but their broadcast turned the trick for many of the more troublesome civilians. The news that an attack by the Germans was eminent was more than enough for many of them. Several promptly quit and went ashore with demands in hand that they be returned to the safety of America as soon as feasible, if not before. Of those that remained, most would do as well as could be expected of basically untrained civilians. This action had finally forced the hand of the US Army. The departed civilians were soon replaced by soldiers, who though they weren't sailors were infinitely more reliable than the men who had recently departed.

The Army's final naval contribution to the effort would eventually total 74 smaller tugs and 6 larger ones. Many of the tug crews, both civilian and military were naturally inexperienced in long distance towing and/or deficient in nautical knowledge. But, after the departure of some of the less dependable civilians, it was hoped that the remaining crews would prove to be more reliable under fire. Several tugs, including some manned by civilians would get lost on their way to the invasion. Many of those would end up being captured by the Germans.

Now we will cover some of the smaller, but possibly even more important portions of the project. While they were not as massive or as recognizable as the *Phoenix,* they were in fact the heart and soul of Mulberry.

The most expensive and complicated part of the prefabricated harbor was the floating roadway which was to be codenamed "*Whale*". It was actually a flexible steel bridge that was supported by floating pontoons. It was connected at its seaward end to what were known as Lobnitz pier-heads. Ships could then tie up directly to the piers and discharge their cargo, which could then be trucked ashore.

A Whale roadway

The roadways themselves were built in 480-foot-long sections with 80-foot spans between pontoons. This was considered to be the optimum size for towing. Their construction would eventually consume more than 60,000 tons of steel.

Technically the pier-heads were part of the *Whale*, but their crews considered them separate entities and called them *Spuds*. That was actually the nomenclature for the telescopic legs on which they rested.

After the British *Mulberry B* was dismantled in December, several sections of the *Whales* were salvaged and used to replace destroyed bridges in France, Holland and Belgium. This eased the demand for the prefabricated "Bailey" bridge, which was custom-made for the job. The Bailey would then be more readily available for use by combat engineer units closer to the frontlines.

Examples of Whales are still in use around Western Europe

The pontoons upon which the roadways rested were known as "*Beetles*". They received their code name from their resemblance to that insect when it was floating on the water. As originally designed, they were to have been constructed of steel and they weighed in at 16 tons apiece. It was estimated that it would take approximately 460 *Beetles* to complete both harbors.

As the program progressed it was determined that such construction would require more than 7,000 tons of steel. That amount could be ill afforded in view of the 60,000 tons that had already been budgeted for the construction of the roadways alone. Since the concept for *Mulberry* had first been conceived, one of the main concerns had been the amount of steel that it would consume. Many of its backers were becoming increasingly reluctant to approach the British high command with demands for yet more building material. Support for the program wasn't that strong within the British hierarchy to begin with. If the cost continued to escalate, there was always the possibility of *Mulberry* being down-sized or even eliminated.

At a time when contractors were scrambling to find steel to build everything from battleships to helmets, the utmost care had to be taken when deciding steel allocations. The crux of the problem was that no matter how much complaining and begging went on there was only so much of the vital metal to go around. Every single ton was critical to the Allied war effort. Alternative solutions would have to be found wherever possible.

The alternative, in the case of the *Beetles,* was a plan to build the majority of them with concrete. Somewhat surprisingly, the concept wasn't all that new. Concrete cargo ships had been built and used during World War I. They had functioned well enough, although they did have their issues with durability.

Whale roadway resting upon steel Beetles

A concrete Beetle pontoon

The main problems that arose with the concrete *Beetle* proto-types were excessive weight and the same durability issues that had troubled the concrete ships of the previous war. After much experimenting, a lighter concrete model was created. Even with the new improved design the concrete pontoons would weigh 19-tons as compared to the 16-tons of the original steel proto-type. They met the weight limitations and load carrying requirements, but the durability problem was never resolved. The concrete couldn't withstand the mildest collision without suffering severe structural damage.

The pontoons that were to be used in waters with sandy bottoms were anchored using the *kite* anchor developed by Allan Beckett. In areas with rocky bottoms, the *Beetles* were to have adjustable spud legs similar to those on the pier-heads. The spuds allowed the pontoons to be secured to the bottom where the anchors might have failed to find a grip.

Luckily for historians, professional and amateur alike, a group of approximately 30 concrete *Beetles* can still be seen along the riverbank of Southampton Water at Dibden Bay between the Hythe Marina and Husband's Shipyard. For some long-forgotten reason these historic relics did not make the voyage to Normandy and so are still with us, sitting where they were built. There are also several examples still in existence on the beach at Arromanches, France.

The Beetles at Dibden Bay

Surprisingly, one of the most effective and least complicated parts of *Mulberry* was just a group of old ships. They were known as "*Corncobs*" and were scuttled in shallow water for use as block-ships. When used in conjunction with the *Phoenix* caissons, they would form the "*Gooseberry*" fixed breakwater system that would help protect the beaches and the *Whale* roadways from the turbulent waters of the English Channel. Originally, they were to have been merchant ships at least 30 of age, and so would have been near the end of their operational lives. When it was found that the number of vessels fitting that criterion was too few to accomplish the mission, the search was expanded to include obsolete warships and ships that were deemed as too damaged by accident or enemy action to be repaired.

When a sufficient number of ships had been acquired, they were sent to the ports of Rosyth, Methil and Oban in Scotland for modification. This was simply a matter of stripping them of non-essential items, adding ballast to secure them to the bottom when they were scuttled, and installing explosive charges for the scuttling process itself. Two weeks prior to the invasion they were sent to the port of Poole on

Britain's southern coast. For the most part, they made the trip under their own power. This ability to move without outside assistance was a major advantage they had over the caissons which required the use of tugboats.

The inclusion of the *Corncobs* in the *Mulberry* plan was mainly at the instigation of the British Admiralty in the person of Admiral Tennant. The British Army, which had a surprising amount of input into what logically should have been a naval program, was totally against the idea.

The Army claimed that block-ships throughout history had been used as a destructive tool rather than a constructive one. Their main purpose was to limit or stop access to an area, not to build any sort of useful or successful mooring location for shipping. They were just too difficult to control during the scuttling process. There wasn't any way to ensure that they would sink when and where they were supposed to. They pointed out the failure of the Admiralty's own plan during World War I to use block-ships to halt the movement of German submarines to and from their bases at Ostend and Zeebrugge on the North Sea. In that case, the scuttled ships had settled out of position and had caused no more than a minor inconvenience to the submarines.

None the less, the initial testing of the portable harbor theory had proven that a breakwater was required to provide protection for the fragile road system that was to be the heart of *Mulberry*. The disagreement between the British Army and Navy concerned the composition of the protection, not its need. The Army felt that the concrete caissons they were building would suffice. In their opinion, the use of the unwieldy *Corncobs* was unnecessary.

The Admiralty, on the other hand, had serious doubts about the need for the Army's caissons. There were many in the Navy who felt that the concrete behemoths weren't worth the time or the money that would be spent on them.

They insisted that scuttled shipping would perform the same function with far less effort or expense. How much of the confrontation concerning the makeup of the breakwater system that could be attributed to inter-service rivalry would be pure speculation on our part, but the issue had arisen before.

The Navy's insistence that block-ships be included in the program was in truth based on some very solid reasons. Even the most optimistic predictions that had been put forward by the Army, would not provide enough caissons to construct two breakwaters of the hoped-for dimensions. The Army eventually had to agree that block ships would have to be used to supplement the limited number of caissons. Otherwise, the area of protected water would have been so restricted as to be of almost no practical use as a harbor.

The Navy also wanted to have more protected anchorages than the two called for in the original plan. With the addition of block ships to the project, each of the five assault beaches would be provided with its own haven for its vulnerable landing craft. (For a complete listing of the five *Gooseberries* and a partial list of the ships involved see Appendix).

They pointed out that the two planned *Mulberry* harbors were located in the geographic center of the five Allied landing beaches. In the likely event of adverse weather, there could be up to 4,000 small craft on the outer beaches which, even if they had a chance to reach the safety of the *Mulberries*, would find no room within the confines of the harbors once they had arrived. With each beach possessing its own anchorage, shelter would be immediately available and not be located miles away over a storm-tossed sea.

The additional *Gooseberries* would not have to be as elaborate as the two *Mulberries*. They would be constructed entirely of block-ships and wouldn't require any of the scarce caissons, nor would they have any *Whale* roadways. Their main purpose was to provide a safe haven for small craft and calmer surf conditions along the beach itself.

An additional benefit derived from the scuttled ships was that they would provide billets for the crews of the small craft operating in the area. They would also serve as facilities for fueling, first aid, etc. The ships were to be sunk in water so shallow that most of their superstructures would be above even the high tide mark. They would eventually prove to be the most reliable, the cheapest and the least troublesome part of the breakwater system.

Gooseberry Breakwater

Now back to the pier-head portion of the *Whale* roadway. It could be considered one of the most interesting and creative parts of the *Mulberry* system. As mentioned earlier it was technically part of the *Whale* flexible roadway system, but it deserves to have its own part in our story.

The design of the Lobnitz pier-head was based on a vessel named LUCAYAN that had been built by Lobnitz and Company of Renfrew, Scotland in 1923 for use in the Bahamas. This combination rock crusher and dredge rested on three adjustable legs, or spuds as they were called, that were lowered to the sea floor. These spuds could be operated manually or with the release of a clutch they would allow the craft to actually rise and fall freely with the tides. This was a definite improvement over Churchill's earlier idea for a floating pier.

The dredge LUCAYAN

When company owner Henry Pearson Lobnitz was approached by the Navy about the design, he felt that there would be no problem modifying the 3-legged dredger into a 4-legged pier-head. But due to the inability of the Lobnitz Company to produce a prototype in time, the contract was transferred to the company of Alexander Findlay and Company in Motherwell.

The completed pier-heads would weigh about 1,100 tons each and would measure 200 feet by 60 feet. As with all the major *Mulberry* components, they would have to be towed across the Channel. When they were in position off the Normandy coast, the legs would then be lowered to the sea bottom. They could then be utilized as a secure base for attaching the seaward ends of the floating roadways. Within the pier-head were several watertight compartments that would provide storage facilities as well as living accommodations for its crew of 22.

Spud pier-head preparing for movement from Britain to Normandy

The completed pier-heads would weigh about 1,100 tons each and would measure 200 feet by 60 feet. As with all the major *Mulberry* components, they would have to be towed across the Channel. When they were in position off the Normandy coast, the legs would then be lowered to the sea bottom. They could then be utilized as a secure base for attaching the seaward ends of the floating roadways. Within the pier-head were several watertight compartments that would provide storage facilities as well as living accommodations for its crew of 22.

When finally positioned off Normandy they would anchor two different types of piers. The stores pier was formed by three *Whales* leading from the shore out to series of interconnected pier-heads that were placed parallel to the shoreline. Large freighters could then be moored alongside the pier-heads and unloaded. From there, the cargo could be trucked onto the *Whales* and then to shore.

Spud pier heads with attached Whale roadways.

The second type of pier was called the LST pier. The pier-heads used on this pier were modified with pontoon ramps, code named "*Buffers*", which allowed landing craft to be beached and unloaded directly onto the pier-head. Further modifications allowed both the lower and upper decks of LSTs to be unloaded at the same time. This greatly decreased the time required to discharge the vessel's cargo. In this design the pier-head was placed at the end of a single *Whale* roadway.

LST pier head with attached Buffer.

The final part of *Mulberry* that we will delve into in some detail is the "*Bombardon*". This problem child of the *Mulberry* family received its code name in an attempt to mislead German military intelligence into believing that it had something to do with anti-aircraft operations.

There were probably several more colorful and less printable names used by the crews that had to deal with it, but we will use the official one.

As opposed to the fixed breakwaters which consisted of the caissons and block-ships, the *Bombardons* were to form a floating breakwater. They were to be linked together and moored about 3 miles offshore. When in position, they would serve as a first line of defense against the waves of the less than friendly Channel waters. The theory was that they would also provide an anchoring area for larger cargo ships while they were awaiting their turn at the piers within the more protected waters of the *Gooseberries*.

Several even more unusual and creative ideas had been investigated and discarded before the *Bombardon* design was finally chosen. One was to lay a miles-long perforated air line that lay on the sea floor. It would theoretically expel massive quantities of air bubbles that would hopefully have a calming effect on the wave action of the surface.

Another concept was a series of sausage-shaped rubber balloons that would be connected and anchored off-shore. Even though this inflatable barrier proved to be completely useless in action, it did lead its designer Robert Lochner to develop what became the *Bombardon*.

Construction of the Bombardon

Although the individual *Bombardons* displaced 2,000 tons of water, they were constructed with only 300 tons of steel each and they were

200 feet long. When viewed from the end they were crucifix shaped. With their dimensions, they somewhat resembled battering rams. That's a little ironic when you consider that is exactly what they became when they helped destroy the American *"Mulberry A"* during a major storm that occurred on June 19th.

Remnants of a Bombardon after the storm

Initially 75 units had been ordered, but due to a change in the planned layout of the two *Mulberry* harbors, that number was increased to 115. The order was again changed in February 1944 when it was reduced to 93 because of a severe steel shortage. Even with the reduction in numbers, the *Bombardons* would consume almost 28,000 tons of the precious metal. That steel would have been better used to construct more than 1,700 steel *Beetle* pontoons. With those additional pontoons, both *Mulberries* could have been completed without being forced to use the less suitable concrete models.

Any chance the *Bombardons* had of doing their job, and there were many who doubted that could have ever happened, was thrown away by improper placing of the barriers off the invasion beaches. At almost the last minute, Royal Navy Admiral Bertram Ramsay, Commander of the *"Neptune"* (naval) portion of *"Overlord"*, decided to place the *Bombardons* in a single line rather than the accepted double line that had been used during testing. This decision increased the size of the protected anchorage, but it also reduced the efficiency of *Bombardon* concept itself. Added to this was the fact that instead of the designed maximum depth of 7 fathoms (35 feet), the *Bombardons* were actually anchored in waters 11-13 fathoms (66-78 feet) deep, which was well beyond the acceptable limits of their mooring system.

As mentioned earlier, during the storm which occurred on June 19th, they broke away from their moorings and, in the case of the American facility, ran amok. Rampaging *Bombardons* would cause eventually cause more damage to the American *Mulberry A* and nearby moored shipping than did the stormy waters alone.

An investigation by the British Admiralty after the storm came to the conclusion that faulty bolt connections rather than poor mooring procedures were to blame. A conclusion that was hardly surprising seeing as the Navy had been responsible for the mooring.

The one major American contribution to *Mulberry* was the "*Rhino*" ferry. It was based on what was called a Naval Lighter (NL) pontoon that had been invented by USN Captain John N. Laycock. The pontoons were to be filled with compressed air and connected together to form rafts measuring 42x176 feet. These rafts, when equipped with an overall surface covering and propelled by outboard motors, were capable of carrying up to 40 wheeled and tracked vehicles between ships off-shore and the beach. The *Rhinos* could also be linked together to form a causeway for unloading cargo and troops off small craft that couldn't land directly on the beach due to heavy surf conditions. The Americans would have 72 *Rhinos*, which had been towed from Britain by LSTs, available off their two beaches after the initial landings.

Rhino ferry

On the other side of the Channel, bickering afflicted the German services just as it did the Allies. In fact, it was carried to even greater heights by the Germans. In some cases it was to prove deadly. In others it was so ridiculous that under less serious circumstances it would have been almost comical. For an example, command of the larger artillery pieces that had been emplaced along the coast to defend against the upcoming Allied invasion was divided between the German Army and Navy. The Navy was in charge while the guns fired at targets out to sea, but as soon as they fired targets ashore they reverted to Army control. If they were alternating between shore and sea objectives, the confusion would have bordered on the ludicrous. This bizarre situation would lead to many unnecessary and costly setbacks for the German defenders.

For once, the Americans didn't suffer the same problems that caused so many headaches for the British. Their portion of *Mulberry* luckily did not have the inter-service issues that continually plagued the British. The American *Mulberry A* was a Navy operation from start to finish. The American Army had only a minor involvement in the project, and that's the way they wanted it. This isn't to say that the Yanks didn't suffer many of the same afflictions that affected the British military; they just didn't surface in the case of *Mulberry*.

If the US Navy had been given an option on its command of the American *Mulberry*, they would probably have taken a pass. Its senior commanders were less than thrilled with the entire concept of a prefabricated harbor, but they had been given responsibility for the American portion and they would begrudgingly do their job. In the Navy's opinion, the concept was not only flawed, it wasn't needed.

One issue that the Americans would have with the program was what they considered the somewhat complacent attitude of the British concerning construction deadlines. In America, deadlines were made to be met if at all possible, whereas in Britain it seemed they were treated with a bit more flexibility.

What the Americans didn't appreciate was that the British were even more concerned about the potentially disastrous failure to complete the project in time than they were. They just handled it differently. The entire concept had been their idea, so they naturally felt additional pressure to see it through to a successful and timely conclusion. It was simply their nature not to exhibit their anxieties and concerns in a public fashion. They would deal with their difficulties as they had for centuries, behind closed doors, privately.

The problems they faced would have seemed almost insurmountable to even the most optimistic member of their planning staff. At this stage of the war there was a very serious shortage of skilled laborers, such as welders and electricians. These would have been essential for the building of the more complex components of *Mulberry*. Also, several years of full throttle wartime construction had depleted the available supply of materiel to complete *Mulberry*. This placed additional restrictions on the designs and the construction techniques to be used.

The issues of labor and material were dealt with by a combination of compromise and negotiation. What couldn't be borrowed or bargained for had to be modified or eliminated. Dealing with everything from labor unions to the government bureaucracy would cause the men of *Mulberry* many a sleepless night. Considering all the potentially disastrous obstacles they had to deal with, it was one of the minor miracles of the war that the British finished the construction of *Mulberry* in time.

That question of time that was probably the biggest problem to be dealt with after the program had been accepted by Allied High Command. There was never enough of it. Nearly every phase of *Mulberry* construction was completed behind schedule. Even the testing of many of the completed components often wasn't accomplished until weeks, and sometimes days before the invasion.

This meant that the Allies couldn't even be sure if the heart of *Mulberry* was sound. The initial connecting of a *Whale* roadway to its Lobnitz pier-head wouldn't even take place until May 24, 1944, about two weeks prior to the invasion. Until that event took place, the feasibility the entire project was in question.

That critical test finally took place off the Isle of Wight near Portsmouth, on the southern coast of Britain. Unfortunately, during the test it was determined that when an LST attempted to dock against the pier-head, its bow doors could not be opened. Without the ability to unload LSTs properly, over 50% of *Mulberry* would be no more than scrap metal. This discovery at such a late date threw the entire program into a panic. When further testing revealed even more problems, it was decided that several modifications would have to be made before D-Day. The most important alteration involved the LST docking difficulties. Luckily, the solution to the problem was a fairly straightforward one. A portion of their bow doors would be cut off. This relatively simple procedure would allow them to open the doors and disembark their cargos onto the pier heads as planned.

There would be more issues to deal with in *Mulberry's* future, but at least it was finally completed. Now, hopefully, it could carry out its mission.

GETTING MULBERRY AFLOAT

In January of 1944, USN Captain Augustus Dayton Clark was assigned to the command of Task Force 128. This was unit would be responsible for the assembling, as well as the operation of the American *Mulberry "A"* off Saint-Laurent-sur-Mer, Normandy.

Clark was an Annapolis graduate. His military career had seen him serve as Captain of the presidential yacht and also as a Presidential aide. His military records also listed a variety of relatively minor staff positions. During his somewhat pedestrian military career, he had apparently performed his duty well enough to achieve the rank of captain, but otherwise had failed to distinguish himself. The main reason he had been given this assignment was that he was about the only available officer who would accept it. In fact, he had actively lobbied for it, for it represented an opportunity for command that might otherwise have eluded him.

Undoubtedly there would be many times in the future when he probably regretted the effort that he had expended to gain his command. It was such a unique proposition that there were no precedents to help guide him in his decision making. Everything concerning *Mulberry* was experimental and unknown. No one was absolutely sure about anything pertaining to it. Even its strongest proponents harbored serious doubts about its viability and would be holding their collective breaths until it was up and running.

His position as commander of TF128 was also complicated by the fact that he had several senior commanders that he had to answer to. Whenever there was a conference or demonstration concerning *Mulberry*, each and every one of them required Clark to be present. This severely limited the time he had available train and organize his command.

The two most senior commanders that he had to concern himself with were Admirals Ramsay and Stark. The Royal Navy's Admiral Bertram Ramsay was Allied Naval Commander Expeditionary Force (ANCXF). He apparently didn't have much faith in the *Mulberry* concept from the beginning and he seems to have limited his involvement with the program as much as he could. Considering the scope of the "*Neptune*" operation, he probably felt that he had far more important issues to deal with than a disposable harbor which he in large part considered extraneous to the entire operation.

Ramsay's previous experience during the war had included overall command of the Allied evacuation of Dunkirk in May of 1941. He also had served as deputy commander of the Allied naval forces during the Allied landings in North Africa "*Operation Torch*" in 1942 and as commander of the naval forces supporting the British landings on Sicily in 1943. He was destined to die in a plane crash outside of Paris in January of 1945. Eisenhower would later describe him and Royal Air Force Chief Air Marshal Trafford Leigh-Mallory, Commander of the Allied Expeditionary Air Force, as his two least favorite subordinates. This is somewhat surprising in view of the fact that he also had under his command two rather independent and egotistical gentlemen named Field Marshal Bernard Montgomery and General George Patton.

The senior US Navy officer that Clark had to answer to was Admiral Harold Stark, Commander US Naval Forces Europe (COMNAVEU). Fortunately for Clark, Stark seemed to prefer staying at his headquarters at Number 20 Grosvenor Square in London than spending time dealing with the nuts and bolts of his command. For the most part, Admiral Stark seems to have left the daily operations to his Chief of Staff, Commodore Howard Flanigan. The general disinterest exhibited by these two officers towards *Mulberry* at least partially reduced two potential command headaches for Clark. But he had plenty of others.

The first was USN Admiral Alan Kirk, Commander of Task Force 122 and Commander of the Western Naval Task Force. TF-122 was composed of all the American naval forces actually involved in *Neptune-Overlord* off *Omaha* and *Utah* beaches. He would be the senior USN commander at sea off Normandy on D-Day. Under his command were a total of 931 ships and the American share of the 2,606 landing craft that would participate in the landings on all the beaches.

Kirk was by many reports an ambitious officer who irritated both his superiors, as well as his subordinates. He must have performed his duties well though, for by the end of the war he was a full admiral. He died in 1963.

Under Kirk was USN Admiral John L. Hall, commander of the 11th Amphibious Force off *Omaha* beach. He was to be one of the most vocal opponents of the *Mulberry* program and would continue to be so well after the war. Captain Clark would seldom have occasion to look forward to a conference with this most troublesome of his superiors.

Hall didn't restrict himself to annoying his subordinates. His superiors, both British and American were also to be recipients of his strongly held opinions. During the invasion of Sicily, the previous year, he and Kirk had been equals, both had commanded task forces. Now he felt that he, not Kirk, should have been given command of TF-122. The injustice of being forced to serve under someone he considered less qualified than himself naturally wore on him and probably affected his relationships, as well his decision making. He felt no compunction about voicing any complaints that he might have about anything that he felt fell within his jurisdiction, or without for that matter.

One of his many grievances concerned the decision not to grant him tactical control of the Air Forces over his area. He was of the opinion that as commander of that portion of front, he should be in control of all forces operating within that area. The Royal Air Force and the US Air Force felt otherwise. They refused to allow either Navy to exercise any control, tactical or otherwise, over the operations of their airplanes. They were already less than happy about the forced disruption of their strategic campaigns against Germany, and they saw no reason why they should sacrifice anymore than they already had.

Hall was also officially reprimanded for strongly voicing his opinion about what he considered a completely inadequate amount of pre-invasion bombardment by the naval forces off-shore. As a Navy man, he was in favor of bombardments that lasted for days or weeks, much like those conducted in the Pacific. It had previously been decided by higher authority that the element of surprise was more crucial than a pre-landing bombardment of that length. He was reminded through official channels of his position in the chain of command and that his job was to carry out his superior's orders, not argue with them.

He also had several heated discussions with Admiral Ramsay over the strict orders issued by SHAEF not to beach and "dry-out" the LSTs. Ramsay feared that they would be damaged and thus lost to future operations. In this Ramsay was completely wrong. The LST had been designed with just such an operation in mind. Any danger that the landing craft could have been damaged on a rocky shoreline had been discounted due to pre-invasion reconnaissance activities by Allied commandoes that had determined the suitability of the beaches for landing craft. The flat sandy bottom along that portion of the coastline was ideal for beaching the LSTs. After the storm of June 19th had all but destroyed *Mulberry "A"*, the Americans had no choice but to use that very procedure. The LSTs were beached constantly and suffered no ill effects. The only down side to the practice will be discussed later.

Hall continued to be an irritant to his superiors even after the successful conclusion of the invasion. His after-action report dated September 22, 1944, contained many criticisms of the way the operation had been handled. Among many other topics, he stated that "Because of the vulnerability of its floatation equipment and the general unseaworthiness of the entire vehicle the DD (duplex-drive) tank is not a practicable weapon for use in assault landings on open beaches". The DD tank, an example of the specialized armor developed by the British specifically for D-Day, will be covered in more detail later in this work.

If Hall, as Commander of the *Omaha* Assault Force, was of that same opinion prior to the assault, he was obligated to have modified the operational orders for the type. Many lives, both at sea and ashore, might have been saved if he had done so. If on the other hand, it was merely a case of hindsight, he might have considered shouldering his share of the blame in ignoring the possibly deadly deficiencies of the amphibious tank concept. Hall, much like his superior Kirk, tended to be very opinionated and bothersome to almost everyone, but again was apparently an able enough naval officer who performed his duties well enough to retire as a full Admiral in 1953. He would die in 1978.

Hall's counterpart off *Utah*, the other American beach, was Rear Admiral Donald P. Moon. Moon was involved with Clark and his Mulberry because the *Gooseberry* breakwater that was to be constructed off *Utah* beach was technically part of *Mulberry "A"*. Moon is a rather sympathetic figure in this story. He didn't assume command of Force "U" (*Utah*) until March 6, 1944, a mere three months before the invasion. Of all the major commanders involved in D-Day, he had the least amount time to familiarize himself with the immense and intricate plan that was *Neptune/Overlord*. By many accounts he felt somewhat overwhelmed by his responsibility as commander of half of the American assault force. The loss of two valuable LSTs and several hundred assault troops in the last training exercise (*Operation Tiger"*) before the invasion further increased his uneasiness concerning his part in the upcoming action.

Immediately after the conclusion of *Neptune* he received orders appointing him as commander of a portion of the Allied naval forces involved in *Operation Anvil/Dragoon*, the assault on Southern France which was set for August. During preparations for that invasion at his headquarters in Naples, Italy Moon committed suicide. According to witness' reports he had been distraught over being given an assignment similar to Normandy and again not having enough time to prepare and train his units. He was to be the only US Navy flag officer to commit suicide during the war.

Another "boss" that Clark had to answer to was USN Rear Admiral John Wilkes, Commander Landing Craft and Bases Europe. The SeaBee (CB-construction battalion) personnel that were needed to assemble and operate *Mulberry "A"* had to be borrowed from Wilkes' command, so he demanded that he have a say in the operation.

Wilkes had commanded Submarine Squadrons 5 & 20 earlier in the war in the Pacific Theater. He had also commanded the USN cruiser BIRMINGHAM during the invasion of Sicily the previous year. He would serve as ComLanCraBEu (Commander Landing Craft, Bases Europe) from August 1943 until June 25, 1944.

On the 25th of June he was appointed as Commander US Ports and Bases, France. After the war he would serve as Commander Submarines Atlantic Fleet until 1948. He then became Commander US Naval Forces, Germany. He remained at that post until he retired.

This would have been plenty of "chiefs" to Clark's "indian", but the British felt obligated to add one more. That would be Royal Navy Rear Admiral William G. Tennant, who would serve as Rear Admiral *Mulberry/PLUTO* (**P**ipe **L**ine **U**nder **T**he **O**cean). Tennant was to be in charge of towing of the *Mulberry* components to Normandy and would command the overall operations of both harbors.

The "towing" portion of Tennant's assignment description would seemingly point the finger of blame in his direction for the previously mentioned failure to secure sufficient tugboats to tow *Mulberry* across the Channel. But, to be fair he could have delegated that responsibility to someone further down the chain of command who then dropped the ball.

The *PLUTO* portion of Tennant's command was another little-known operation. It consisted of a series of flexible fuel lines that were to be laid on the bottom of the English Channel much like a Trans-Atlantic communications cable. They were to be used to move fuel from Britain to ports along the French Channel coast to help alleviate the need to use shipping for the same purpose after the invasion.

PLUTO on its storage spool

Captain Clark also had one major worry that had nothing to do with his convoluted chain of command. At first glance, the issue would seem so basic a requirement for success that it's almost incredible that it was over-looked. Again, the British insistence on a divided command structure was the root of the problem. It was in large part due to Clark's exertions that the problem was resolved and disaster averted.

Almost since the first day of his assuming command he had berated almost anyone he could corner with all the reasons why *Mulberry* might possibly never see the Norman coast. Specifically, he had no faith in the ability of the British Royal Engineers to actually deliver on their promise to raise *Mulberry* from its resting place off the British coast. He had an all-consuming fear that he would be left sitting off the beaches of Normandy waiting for a portable harbor was still stuck in the mud off the southern coast of Britain. He had become so troublesome that his complaints were finally brought to the attention of Admiral Harold Stark.

Stark himself had a somewhat checkered past. He had been serving as Chief of Naval Operations in Washington D.C. at the time of the Japanese attack on Pearl Harbor on December 7, 1941. At the time, there had been some debate over how much responsibility he should bear for that tragedy. Early in 1942, President Roosevelt had transferred him to this brand-new post in Britain. There had always been a question in some people's minds about whether this action had been taken to remove a possible embarrassment to the administration and place it in an unimportant backwater assignment, or if it was really a worthwhile assignment for a former CNO.

By 1944, there was definitely nothing unimportant or backwater about commanding the US Naval Forces in Europe. It was rumored that Stark in his new position tended to be more of a political figure than an actual commander. At this point in his career, he was a man who was more at ease operating in the company of Kings and Prime Ministers than he was dealing with the ever-growing elements of his command. But as the US Navy's top Admiral in Europe, he still had a number of responsibilities that couldn't be delegated out. One of those was turned out to be determining whether there was any justification in the complaints being voiced so loudly and so often by one of his subordinates.

When Stark initially made his inquiries with the British as to any problems which might occur when *Mulberry* was raised from its shallow water storage areas, he was informed that the Royal Engineers were in charge. There was no doubt the job would be done and done right. The Royal Engineers had been accomplishing their assigned missions for centuries and there was no reason to doubt them now. As far as the British were concerned, that was the end of the discussion.

This was good enough for Stark, but not for Clark. He kept up his incessant complaining and continued to badger everyone, British and American alike. So when one of the leading salvage experts in the US Navy, Captain Edward Ellsberg, was assigned to Stark's command it appeared to be a golden opportunity to finally shut up the troublesome Captain Clark. A favorable report from Ellsberg concerning the recovery situation at Selsey Bill, which was the main storage area for *Mulberry*, would hopefully dispel the doubts that seemed to plague the man. Unfortunately, for everyone except Captain A. Dayton Clark, Ellsberg's report was not what Commander US Naval Forces Europe had hoped for.

Feeling somewhat sidetracked from his original assignment, that of planning and constructing port facilities at Quiberon Bay on the

Brittany coast of France after the Normandy landings, Ellsberg had been assured that this new job was a temporary one. He was merely to check out the British salvage preparations for *Mulberry* and report back to London.

When Ellsberg arrived at Selsey Bill, on what he personally considered a wild-goose chase, his first impression was that he was looking at a sunken city. Sitting in the mud just offshore was nearly 600,000 tons of caissons, roadways and piers. To his trained eye, it was more than half a million tons of shipping that would have to be raised from the bottom in a matter of days according to a very tight schedule. The job was far more immense than anything he had ever considered possible.

After spending most of the morning trying to decipher the totally confused British command structure ashore, he inquired what facilities would be available for the upcoming recovery operation. He was informed that two Dutch coastal freighters located just off shore would be sufficient for the job. They had pumps aboard that were more than powerful enough to complete the task.

Keeping in mind that Stark's Chief of Staff, Commodore Howard Flanigan, had given him strict orders to keep his opinions to himself and that under no circumstances was he to upset or offend the British, he hid what were becoming serious doubts in his mind concerning the operation. He asked if he could get a ride out to inspect the pumps aboard the Dutch vessels. The British said they would be glad to oblige, but they had a problem. Their problem was that neither the British Navy nor Army had a boat in which he could travel offshore! The only boats available were the property of the US Navy and apparently, they were under the command of a rather obnoxious, in British opinion, USN lieutenant by the name of Fred Barton.

Ellsberg had a rather difficult time locating Barton until he remembered that part of the British description of Barton was his total lack of military bearing. After dealing with a parade of British officers in full dress uniforms, he expanded his search to a group of obvious Americans who were definitely not in the proper uniform of the day. When he spotted a large man dressed in a sweatshirt and shorts bellowing through a bullhorn, he knew he had his Barton. Once Ellsberg had met with the "obnoxious" Lieutenant Barton, transportation was arranged.

After boarding the flagship of the Dutch pump boats, he introduced himself to the British Army captain in charge of the pumping operation and explained his mission. He was proudly taken below decks and shown the pumps. When he first laid eyes on them he was dumbstruck. For a variety of technical reasons, he knew beyond a shadow of a doubt that there was no way those pumps were going to perform as promised. For the lack of anything better to say, he told the Army captain that they looked big enough for almost any job. He then asked where the Army had gotten them. He was informed that they were sewage pumps that had been originally designed for the construction of London's new sewage system, a project which had been put on hold for the duration of the war. Upon further investigation Ellsberg found that virtually every component of the pumping system had originally been built for some other function. The haphazard arrangements that had been made for such an important task left him stunned.

Captain Clark had found an ally. This wasn't a wild goose chase; it was a disaster waiting to happen.

After returning to shore, Ellsberg immediately headed back to London to report his findings. He filed his report that night knowing that it did not contain the conclusions that his superiors had desired. He returned to his room and waited for the storm to hit. The next day he was called into Commodore Flanigan's office and debriefed. Although Flanigan was definitely less than thrilled with Ellsberg's report, he refused to contest the findings within it. He simply said that he would pass it along to Admiral Stark. He then directed Ellsberg to return to Selsey Bill and await further orders.

He left London more than a little disappointed and confused. He had considered his job at Selsey Bill finished. He had been looking forward to getting on with the planning for the Quiberon Bay project and now it looked as though he might never get there.

After his return to Selsey Bill, he spent most of that first day trying to think of something that would justify his being there. He soon learned that the US Navy had a state-of-the-art salvage tug, the DIVER, on site. He then decided to try and accomplish something while he was waiting for a more worthwhile assignment. After clearing it with the omnipotent Lieutenant Barton, he asked for a test to be run using the pumps that were aboard the American boat. During that test it was found that even with all the water pumped out of the test caisson, it refused to budge from the bottom. The problem was that suction had been created by letting the flat-bottomed caisson sit in the mud for an extended period of time.

Ellsberg then devised a system that forced high pressure water under the caisson and which broke the mud's grip. Now, the problem was to get the British Army to use the system or better yet put a more qualified group, preferably the US Navy in Ellsberg's opinion, in charge of the operation.

Word was soon received at Selsey Bill that Prime Minister Churchill and his entourage would be arriving on an inspection tour to pass judgment of the preparations for raising *Mulberry*. Although this inspection when it occurred appeared to several of those present, including Ellsberg, to be short and rather casual, it apparently made quite an impression on Churchill.

Upon returning to Number 10 Downing Street, Churchill made the decision that the Navy was much more qualified to handle such an operation than the British Army. Unfortunately, in Ellsberg's opinion, the Navy he meant was the British Navy. This should have come as no surprise as this was a British operation located in Britain. British national pride couldn't be expected to stand for a British baby to be delivered by an American doctor.

As far as Ellsberg was concerned, this latest development had resulted in the completion of his assignment. He had found the problems within the Mulberry program and they had been resolved, although not completely to his satisfaction. He felt justified in anticipating a return to headquarters in London and to reacquainting himself with the Quiberon project.

Much to his chagrin, the next orders he received stated that he was to remain in Selsey Bill and serve as a consultant to the new British commander of the salvage operation. He felt distinctly uncomfortable with his new duty. If he had been in command the last thing that he would have wanted was a British "consultant" getting in the way and confusing the situation. After voicing his displeasure with the assignment to Chief of Staff Flanigan, he was officially informed that his opinion didn't really matter. Those were his orders and he was to carry them out.

Eventually, when he met the new man in charge of the *Mulberry* recovery program, Commodore MacKenzie of the Royal Navy, he was duly impressed, although he was still not comfortable with the situation. They had never met personally, but they were known to each other by reputation. Ellsberg had gained almost world-wide renown for his salvage operations in the Red Sea and the Mediterranean during the present conflict, whereas Mackenzie had been responsible for salvaging the Imperial German Fleet after it had been scuttled at Scapa Flow in 1919.

While Ellsberg was on one of his many trips to Stark's headquarters in London in his never-ending attempt to procure what he considered a more worthwhile assignment, he learned the story behind Churchill's unexpected inspection of the situation at Selsey Bill.

According to the rumor mill, Admiral Stark had used his personal and political connections to instigate the British Prime Minister's decision to take time from his busy schedule and travel to the wilds of Selsey Bill. It had been the British King, George VI, who had suggested to Churchill that it might be beneficial if he were to make the trip.

Stark had found himself in somewhat of a quandary when he received Ellsberg's negative report. His previous inquiries into the ability of the Royal Engineers to perform their assignment of recovering of the caissons from the sea floor had raised the ire of more than a few high-ranking British military and government officials. If he was to reiterate his previous concerns, the repercussions might be felt all the way to the White House and end what was left of his military career. Fortunately, Stark came to the conclusion that there was more at stake than his personal job security, so he had pressed on.

It seems that Stark and the British King were actually old shipmates. During the First World War, Stark had been assigned as an observer aboard the Royal Navy flagship IRON DUKE. While aboard, he made the acquaintance of the future King who was serving as a ship's officer. The two became friends and had remained so throughout the years. Stark had reportedly used that friendship to arrange an appointment with the King, thus bypassing the many disgruntled bureaucrats and senior British military officers who might have stood in his way. During that meeting, the King was informed that there were serious concerns among the Americans that *Mulberry* could succeed under the present conditions. Apparently, the King felt that there was some justification for those concerns and soon made his suggestion to Churchill.

In bringing British Royal attention to a potentially disastrous problem that could have altered the outcome of the Allied invasion of France Stark had gone a long way towards making up for any past mistakes, real or implied, that he might have made while serving as USN Chief of Naval Operations. By going over the heads of everyone in the British government and the British military he undoubtedly didn't make a lot of friends, but there were going to be thousands of Allied soldiers who were going to have vital supplies that they may have had to do without if *Mulberry* had been left sitting in the mud off Selsey Bill.

THE AMERICAN MULBERRY

Now that one of Dayton's most pressing concerns over his command had been addressed, he could now focus on the more usual issues of assembling and operating his *Mulberry "A"* off the beaches of Normandy.

The American harbor was originally to have consisted of 34 of the caisson breakwaters, with an additional 19 to be used as spares to replace those lost due to German fire or bad weather. Due to time constraints the 34 had been reduced to 31 and the spares were eliminated all together.

According to the planned layout for *"A"*, it would have six Lobnitz pier-heads, three ½-mile long roadways and more than three miles of breakwater made up of caissons and block-ships. Two of the roadways were to be capable of carrying loads of up to 25-tons, while the third could support up to 40-tons. The smaller capacity of the first two could accommodate most vehicles, but the larger one would be required for off-loading tanks and heavy artillery. It had been estimated by the invasion planners that *Mulberry "A"* would be able to 5,000 tons of supplies per day when completed.

When the day of the invasion finally arrived Captain Dayton found that his problems were far from over. Early on the morning of D-Day he boarded the 110-foot sub chaser SC-1329, which was to serve as his flagship during the construction of *Mulberry "A"*, and there he sat.

It wasn't until the afternoon that the advance *Mulberry* units finally received orders to proceed on their voyage to Normandy.

Soon after joining the conveyor belt of Allied shipping headed east, it was discovered that the proper radio code books were not aboard. Any coded messages addressed to the commander of *Mulberry "A"* could not be deciphered. Clark would have no idea of the situation into which he was sailing, or even if the invasion itself had failed. So precise was the timing of every facet of the transit across the English Channel that there was absolutely no possibility of altering course or arranging a rendezvous with another vessel to acquire the needed code books. He had no choice but to continue on and hope for the best.

After a nerve-racking trip he arrived off Normandy. He then made the decision to transfer his headquarters to the larger LSI-414, which presumably possessed the proper code books. He would retain the use of the smaller SC-1329 for use as a more agile vessel to be used on his many inspections and supervising trips around his floating command, but LSI-414 would be his home until the conclusion of his assignment.

His Deputy Commander, Alan Stanford, arrived soon after aboard the SC-1352. That vessel would continue to serve as Stanford's personal flagship while he completed the assembly of the *Gooseberry 1* breakwater off *Utah* beach. That was his primary responsibility as Clark's second-in-command. After the successful completion of that assignment, he would then proceed to *Omaha* where he would assist Clark in the assembly of the complicated roadway system within *Mulberry "A"*.

The Royal Navy's Commander Passmore was to assist the Americans in the laying out of their breakwater off *Omaha*. The most important part of his mission was the verifying and augmenting of the depth soundings reported by the reconnaissance teams prior to the invasion. This would enable the proper placing of the breakwater components. His vessel of choice was the 30-foot survey boat GULNARE. He was accompanied by Captain Clark during the initial part of his assignment.

After returning Clark to his flagship, Passmore returned to the waters off-shore and began placing marker buoys. These were positioned so as to assist in placing the block-ships which were scheduled to be arriving shortly.

After completion, the *Gooseberry 2* portion of *Mulberry "A"* off *Omaha* would be commanded by Lieutenant Commander John Bassett. Bassett had been a well-known tug master in New York Harbor before the war. Bassett, based on his long experience, was of the opinion that he knew better than anyone else how to do his job. This strongly-held belief would lead to many confrontations with the equally opinionated Captain Clark who held the same estimation of his own abilities.

The military unit that was assigned to supply the men for the American *Mulberry* program was the 108th Seabees. Its members would help transport the various *Mulberry* components across the Channel. They would assemble it off *Omaha* beach and then would continue to serve as its operating crew.

The man in charge of scuttling the *Corncobs* (block-ships) at *Gooseberry 2* was USN Commander C.R. Dennen. On D+1, he successfully sank his first block ship; she was the Liberty Ship JAMES IREDELL. Unfortunately, her civilian crew had balked at performing their assigned duties after they came under enemy fire. They had to be replaced by USN personnel who were already on hand to perform other duties. These replacements, although inexperienced, performed their jobs without any further problems. The next two ships to be scuttled were the BAIALOIDE and the GALVESTON. As the GALVESTON settled to the bottom, German artillery fire in the area began to intensify. Several of the crews aboard the *Corncobs* were wounded. This, because of the shortage of trained personnel, was to create further difficulties later in the operation.

In an interesting sidelight, the German artillery observers when viewing the sinking of ships which they had just fired upon naturally assumed that they were responsible. In a propaganda broadcast from Berlin the Germans claimed to have sunk several Allied ships that had ventured too close to shore. They were especially proud of having destroyed a British battleship of the IRON DUKE-class, the CENTURION. CENTURION had in actuality been scuttled just like the rest of the *Corncobs* in *Gooseberry 2* off *Omaha* Beach. She was to serve as the command ship for that unit until her back was broken during the storm of June 19th.

By D+2 *Gooseberry 2* had seven *Corncob* block-ships and three *Phoenix* caissons in place. At this time, Captain Clark received word that one of his *Phoenix* had been lost due to enemy action off Selsey Bill. The first of many adjustments would now have to be made to his harbor. A total of four would be lost while in transit to Normandy. Three were lost to adverse weather conditions and one was destroyed by the Germans.

Over at *Gooseberry 1*, off *Utah* Beach, the first ship to be scuttled was the GEORGE W. WASSON. Due to a shortage of tugboats and the stronger than expected current, WASSON sank out of position. The next ship, the MATT W. RANSOM, also drifted out of her proper position before she sank.

The misplaced ships required the first of the changes to be made at *Gooseberry 1*. It was decided to discard the original plan for one large facility. Two smaller, crescent shaped breakwaters would be based on the two out of position ships. This ended up working so well that during a later inspection by senior officers the new improvised plan received several compliments on its efficiency.

It would be the following day before the next ship, the BENJAMIN CONTE, was scuttled at *Gooseberry 1*. Even though the two British-crewed tugs responsible for placing her in position departed earlier than scheduled due to German shellfire, she managed to settle near her assigned location.

June 9th (D+3) off *Omaha* saw the arrival of the first *Whale* roadways and *Phoenix* caissons from Britain. But, due to the heavy shell-fire in the area, assembly of the *Whales* couldn't begin for 3 more days.

All the *Corncob* block-ships at *Gooseberry 2* were in place by the morning of June 11th (D+5), the last two scuttled being the WEST CHESWALD and the WEST NOHNO. Also, in position were twelve of the *Phoenix* caissons. German shell-fire finally began to slacken enough to enable the placement of the Lobnitz pier-heads. This was the first step in constructing the *Whale* roadways.

Further off-shore, USN Commander L.D. Ard had almost completed the mooring of his *Bombardon* floating breakwater. As with the British facility further to the east, this portion of the American *Mulberry* consisted of twenty-four units stretched out in a mile-long line. In the case of the British *Bombardon,* the commander was C.I Horton of the Royal Navy. Both breakwaters were completed by the 17th.

Bombardons in position

On the same day the USN tugboat PARTRIDGE, while towing a *Whale* from Britain, was sunk by German S-boats.

When *Gooseberry 1,* located off *Utah* beach, was completed on June 13th (D+7), it could accommodate 75 Liberty ships. It had two causeways built of NL pontoons (*Rhinos*), one of which extended beyond the breakwater. The facility would perform well enough to enable the Americans to use it as a major supply base until November.

On the same day the Germans, after apparently finally realizing the significance of the *Mulberries,* began attacking them with aircraft. Most of the Luftwaffe attacks were mounted to drop mines within the harbors themselves. Their weapon of choice was often the "oyster" pressure mine. This little package would just lie on the bottom until the increased water pressure from a ship passing over caused its detonation.

On June 14th (D+8) *Mulberry "A"* was officially declared operational. It had 32 of its 51 breakwater units in place. A causeway built of NL pontoons was now operating and it could handle the smaller landing craft that were being used to move supplies from the larger ships off-shore.

The 14th was also the day the combat engineers cleared out the last of the German anti-boat obstacles on *Omaha* beach. This greatly increased the American's ability to unload directly onto the beach thus easing the work load of the single causeway then in use.

By the evening of June 15th (D+9) the first *Whale* roadway was completed at *Mulberry "A"*. This was three days ahead of schedule, but in the rush to finish the job the Americans had only anchored every sixth supporting pontoon to the seabed. The original design had called for each one of them to be secured. At the time this didn't seem to be a major concern as the weather forecast for the immediate future was favorable.

1630 hours (4:30 pm) on June 16th saw the first operational use of a Lobnitz pier-head at *"A"* when an LST successfully docked on the *"Buffer"* pontoon that served as its landing ramp. The first vehicle off the LST was a DUKW (an amphibious truck). The entire unloading operation took only 38 minutes and unloaded 78 vehicles. The British would eventually claim the record by unloading an LST at their *Mulberry "B"* in just 18 minutes. This made a complete mockery of the 10-12 hours that it would take to unload the same ship if using the beaching and drying out operation preferred by many of the Americans.

The LST responsible for this landmark operation off *Omaha* was Hull Number 543, commanded by USN Lieutenant Robert Fulton Blake. Number 543 had left the port of Southampton the previous day and had been moored off *Omaha* beach since her arrival. After her initial unloading, she returned to Southampton and was reloaded. By the afternoon of the 18th, she had discharged a second shipment of vehicles onto the same pier-head. She was a brand-new vessel and had been built only four months before in Evansville, Indiana.

It was at this time that *Mulberry "A"* underwent an impromptu inspection by a team from the British *Mulberry "B"* which was less than halfway to completion. The British were impressed with the speed with which the Americans had built their harbor. So much so that soon afterwards they replaced the naval commander at their own *Mulberry*.

But, they were also concerned with the lack of proper anchoring of the *Beetle* pontoons at the American facility. Being more familiar with the inconsistencies of the English Channel and its weather patterns they tried to emphasize the importance of properly securing the roadways. Unfortunately, the Americans were more interested in completing a second *Whale* rather than properly finishing the first. They would get to it when they could. By the time the big storm hit on the 19th, they still hadn't finished the job.

It was about this time that our old friend Ellsberg finally made it to Normandy. Immediately after his arrival, he headed directly for Captain Clark's flagship to offer his assistance in any way possible. When he arrived, he found Clark totally distraught over the fact that so many of the heavy duty 38-ton capacity pontoons had been lost in transit that he was unable to construct a *Whale* roadway capable of supporting the weight of tanks. The lighter 25-ton capacity pontoons could support the weight of the cargo trucks, but not that of Sherman tanks.

What he needed from Ellsberg was a solution to his dilemma. Between the two of them they came to the conclusion that by alternating 38-ton and 25-ton pontoons on the same *Whale*, they could possibly create a functional tank roadway.

After retiring to his quarters, Ellsberg spent the night alone with his slide rule. By the end of his study session, he had confirmed that under very severe restrictions their plan could work with literally inches to spare. The tanks would have to maintain a minimum distance of 160 feet between vehicles and their speed couldn't exceed 5 miles per hour.

The next morning, Captain Clark made the decision to go ahead with the modified plan. By the 16th, the makeshift roadway was completed and Ellsberg personally led the first Sherman over it.

That was the same day that due to rough seas; the decision was made to delay the towing of all remaining *Mulberry* components across the Channel. The next day the situation hadn't improved, so for another day critical components sat idle in British harbors 100 miles from where they were needed. The entire project continued to fall further and further behind schedule.

Finally, on the 18th there was a break in the weather. Four *Phoenix* and twenty-four *Whale* tows were immediately dispatched for the Far Shore. These tows would unfortunately be caught in a storm that struck the Channel the 19th. That unexpected tempest would sink eleven of the twenty-eight tows before they could reach their destination. Even with the shortage of components off the invasion beaches, a second 25-ton capacity *Whale* had been opened off *Omaha* beach on June 17th.

Throughout the assembly process enemy actions and accidents had cost the Americans several components of *"A"*. This required an almost continuous changing of the planned layout of the harbor. But both the American and the British adapted their projects to the ever-changing situation and continued to perform their assigned missions with an effort that deserves far more recognition than is sadly the case.

By the end of the day on the 18th, the day before the big storm hit, the Americans had unloaded 314,514 troops, 41,000 vehicles and 116,000 tons of supplies. That put them in an almost dead heat with the British who had brought 314,547 troops, 54,000 vehicles and 102,000 tons of supplies. These numbers made the American and British invasion beaches the first and second busiest ports in all of Europe.

Early in the morning of June 19th the winds began to increase. They eventually reached such velocity that it was deemed too dangerous for the anti-aircraft crews stationed aboard the *Phoenix* caissons to remain at their posts. Later in the morning, the *Whale* roadways began twisting so badly in the turbulent waters that unloading of the shipping off-shore had to be stopped. As dusk at the end of the day some of the caissons began collapsing.

Later that night at *Mulberry "A"* a salvage barge and five British LCTs (landing craft tanks) were hurled by the heavy seas into the roadways. Their crews having lost control of their vessels or had run out of fuel.

The next morning the weather abated somewhat and temporary repairs were made to the some of the damaged units. By that afternoon the conditions again worsened and the beaches were soon littered with many damaged or destroyed landing craft.

The main issue with the landing craft was that they had never been designed to withstand such severe seas. Unlike larger vessels, they were not equipped with anchors. They couldn't secure themselves offshore and ride out the storm. All they could do was circle off the beach and try not to get swamped by the high waves. Once they ran out of fuel, their crews became mere passengers with no control over their charges. They were going to go wherever Mother Nature sent them.

Understandably, some of the landing craft crews panicked and tried to tie up to the *Whales* before they ran out of fuel. Even the very real threat of gunfire from the crews of the *Whales* wasn't enough to dissuade them in their quest for self preservation.

That night the storm intensified and the *Bombardon* breakwaters began breaking loose from their moorings further off-shore. They immediately began drifting towards the shore. They soon began crashing into the inner breakwaters, as well as the anchored shipping outside in the open water. It was later determined that the much of the damage suffered by the caissons of *Mulberry "A"* during the storm was inflicted by runaway *Bombardons*.

Captain Clark's troubles continued as he began to receive reports that several of the *Corncob* block-ships had broken their backs in the heavy seas and had been rendered all but useless. He sent his deputy Stanford to investigate the situation. Stanford, upon boarding the former British battleship CENTURION, which was serving as the centerpiece and flagship of the American *Corncob* fleet, found that she too was succumbing to the pounding waters. After confirming the reports of the damage to the rest of the breakwater, he immediately climbed back aboard his own vessel and began the dangerous voyage back to deliver the bad news to Clark. Minutes after Stanford departed, the CENTURION's keel did indeed snap. She then settled deeper into the mud and waves began crashing over her main deck.

By the night of the 21st, two of the three pier-heads at *"A"* had been lost. Commander Stanford came to the conclusion that the only way to save the last one was to release the clutch control and let the entire structure rise and fall with the action of the waves.

The miserable and terrifying hours in the dark that the crew of that last pier-head must have endured can't really be appreciated by anyone who was not there to suffer through the nightmare. Throughout the night, 15-foot waves slid under them, raising them on a crest and then plunging them into an equally deep trough. As they bounced like a cork in the heavy sea, the uppermost thought in their minds must have been whether the spindly legs of the Lobnitz would hold. If the legs failed, the very next wave could spell their doom.

An additional strain on their nerves was undoubtedly provided by an extra cargo they had aboard. Numerous bodies of dead comrades they had felt compelled to save from the raging sea were stacked like cord wood on the decks of the pier-head. Most of corpses were those of drowned sailors from the multitude of floundered landing craft that were also being ravaged by the storm. The pier-head would survive the ordeal, but those crewmen must have carried the memories of that night until the day they died.

The storm finally began to weaken on the night of the 22nd. At dawn of the 23rd the shaken and exhausted survivors of *Mulberry "A"* crawled out of the wreckage and began to survey the damage. What they found was a chaotic mass of wreckage; the surrounding area was filled with all matter of debris, human as well as material. It looked like the aftermath of a major battle, as indeed it was.

About the only bright light they found on this gloomy morn was that the majority of the *Corncob* block-ships had survived in reasonably good shape. The scuttled ships had not only survived, they had provided life-saving shelter for many of the smaller craft and their crews. Even with the protection of the *Corncobs*, more than 100 landing craft had been destroyed or disabled.

Mulberry "A" after the storm

The storm waters and the rampaging *Bombardons* had destroyed or badly damaged 21 of the 31 *Phoenixes* that had been placed off *Omaha*. Fortunately, those that remained functional, when used in conjunction with the *Corncobs*, were still approximately 50% effective in reducing wave action within the harbor area. All but one the finished *Whale* roadways were completely destroyed and that one was heavily damaged. Upon further examination, it was determined that the majority of the damage the roadways had suffered had been inflicted by out of control landing craft and the renegade *Bombardon*. It was determined that they would probably have survived the storm if not for these factors.

The *Mulberry* harbors had been designed to withstand what were considered to be the average weather conditions for the Channel at that time of year. When the worst storm in 40 years hit, packing wind gusts of up to 70 miles per hour, the harbor had been called upon to exceed its design limits.

The day after the storm had subsided, in what must have been a superhuman effort, 10,000 tons of supplies were unloaded directly onto *Omaha* beach without the benefit of the piers. The surviving breakwaters undoubtedly helped in achieving this almost unbelievable total by reducing wave action along the shore line.

Although he had been receiving reports from his own staff concerning the damage to the *Mulberry* harbor the commander of the American First Army, General Omar Bradley, was constantly demanding more supplies. He was especially concerned about the shortage of artillery shells. These were going to be critical in his upcoming assault on the port of Cherbourg. Finally, on the 22nd and at the end of his patience, he decided to make a personal inspection of the situation off *Omaha*. After viewing the very real devastation that was present, he began to show a bit more understanding for the difficulties that the Navy faced. He still needed his supplies, but he was now more sympathetic towards the plight of the sailors.

After surveying the storm damage, the team in charge of *Mulberry* "A" felt that they could still save part of it. If enough material was salvaged, they felt that it would be possible to renew operations again on a limited schedule. They were supported in this opinion by Captain

Ellsberg, no novice at salvage work himself. Unfortunately, all the personnel that were involved with *Mulberry "A"* were outranked by Commodore W.A. Sullivan. Sullivan had been designated by the US Navy Department as Supervisor of Salvage for the European Theater. As such, he was the man Eisenhower counted on for advice in such matters.

Sullivan had previously "crossed swords" with Ellsberg in the Mediterranean Theater earlier in the war. That prior relationship may have affected some of his subsequent actions. He had never been a strong advocate of the *Mulberry* concept and after receiving an overly optimistic report from his staff concerning the availability of the port facilities at Cherbourg, he made his decision. In line with the recommendations of his staff, he reported to Ike that Cherbourg would be up and running within 3 days of its capture by American forces. This opinion as well as the carnage he had witnessed off *Omaha*, led him to recommend that *Mulberry "A"* be dismantled. Its remnants could then be salvaged and used in the repair of the British *Mulberry "B"*.

This was the final straw for the overwrought Captain Clark. He had lost the project that had all but consumed him for the past 6 months. He became a shell of his former self and was eventually sent back to Britain after being diagnosed as suffering from complete mental and physical exhaustion. He eventually recovered, but never held another command. His replacement during the final phase in the life of *Mulberry "A"* was Commander J.D. Ard, who had been in charge of the *Bombardon* breakwater off *Omaha* beach.

With the decision by Eisenhower to decommission *Mulberry "A"*, the Americans began the task of unloading their supplies directly onto the beach. The majority of American commanders had preferred this method all along. Now they could show their stuff!

In the week following the storm, the Allies would land 26,165 vehicles in France. That sounds impressive until it is noted that the original *Overlord* plan had called for the landing of more than 31,000 in that same period. They also fell behind their projected 110,000-ton target for supplies landed by more than 30,000 tons.

While the Americans had been correct in their doubts about the ability of *Mulberry* to withstand the storms of the English Channel, they had been a little overzealous in their claims concerning their ability to successfully supply the Allied Armies by landing supplies on the beaches.

The Allies would continue to lose ground to their supply requirements even after the British *Mulberry "B"* returned to partial operation on June 30th. Try as they might, they found that it was impossible to provide sufficient materiel to their armies without some sort of harbor facilities, temporary or otherwise. For a variety of reasons, supply issues would continue to plague them until the end of the war in Europe. Those issues will be dealt with in more detail later in the story.

The structural failure of *Mulberry "A"* during the storm was attributed to a number of factors, depending on which of the few references available you might be reading. The British claimed that the Americans had never taken the idea of *Mulberry* seriously and in their rush to complete the project ahead of schedule had failed to anchor the roadways properly to the sea bottom. They blamed the decision by the Americans to anchor alternating pontoons for the disaster. This alternate anchoring scheme, according to the British, had resulted in severe twisting of the roadways and had caused their destruction. The original plan had indeed called for securing all the pontoons to the sea floor, but the Americans had chosen speed over security. The British then pointed to the survival of their own *Mulberry "B"* as an example of how the design would fare when properly assembled and anchored.

The Americans, on the other hand, felt that the failure of the roadways was caused by the fragile design's incapacity to withstand the pounding it received from the drifting landing craft and the *Bombardons* that had run amok during the storm. It wasn't their anchoring procedures that were at fault, it was the design flaws which they had ridiculed from the start. *Mulberry* just wasn't tough enough.

They also questioned the British boasts of how *"B"* had survived the storm. It had been barely half completed when the storm hit. There were fewer components in place to be damaged. *"B"* had also enjoyed the additional protection of the Calvados Reef, which *"A"* had not.

Normally this shallow water just off-shore wouldn't have affected the situation so drastically. In this case though, the storm's somewhat unseasonable approach from the northeast placed the reef in position to dilute the heavy wave conditions.

The usual storm track for that time of year was from the northwest. This information had led to first priority being given during construction to the breakwater protection to the northwest. This procedure had been followed at both harbors, but in the case of the British facility the reef had supplemented the misplaced breakwaters.

The Allied weather forecasters, who had done such an outstanding job up to this point, had failed to predict this new storm for one very understandable reason. It had arrived from the direction of German-occupied Norway. Their ability to observe the weather over the central Atlantic had previously enabled them to formulate extremely accurate forecasts. When they lost that advantage, their prognostications naturally suffered.

Another possible reason for the failure of *"A"* may have been one of unfamiliarity with the equipment. The Americans suffered from an almost complete lack of training in assembling the *Whales* prior to the invasion. They had watched this rather complicated procedure being completed by trained British crews, but had almost no hands-on training. This had been a matter of time constraints, not poor planning. There just wasn't enough time for sufficient practice. The American crews would be shown how to do it and hopefully that would be good enough. When this deficiency is taken into consideration, the fact that *Mulberry "A"* was built at all is a minor miracle.

THE BRITISH MULBERRY

To the east of the American beaches, the British had their own issues concerning *Mulberry*. One of the problems was self-created; it was their scrambled command structure. The division of responsibilities between the Army and the Navy had disrupted the program back in Britain and it didn't get any more efficient after reaching France.

As with the Americans, the movement of *Mulberry* across the Channel went as well as could be expected. The Royal Navy, for its part had delivered *Mulberry* as ordered. It was after reaching the Far Shore that their tribulations began.

Before we delve into those issues that faced *Mulberry "B"*, a little information concerning the backgrounds of the relevant British naval commanders might be of interest.

The counterpart of the USN's Admiral Kirk to the West was Royal Navy Rear Admiral Philip Vian. He had been designated as Commander Eastern Naval Task Force and as such was in charge of all naval matters off the British and Canadian beaches.

Vian had compiled an impressive record earlier in the war. In 1939, he had been the Captain of the destroyer COSSACK when that vessel had captured the German tanker ALTMARK while she was anchored neutral Norwegian waters. The ALTMARK had served as a supply ship for the German "pocket battleship" GRAF SPEE which had operated in the South Atlantic until she was sunk by Royal Navy cruisers off

Argentina. Aboard the ALTMARK were more than 200 British sailors who had survived when their ships had fallen prey to the GRAF SPEE.

Vian had been transferred to the Mediterranean soon after that action. While in that Theater, he had garnered many well-deserved accolades and promotions. After D-Day, his climb up the ladder of Royal Navy's hierarchy would continue and he would finish the war as Commander of the Royal Navy's fleet in the Pacific. He died in 1968 at the age of 74.

The commander of the British *Gold* beach assault was Royal Navy Commodore Cyril E. Douglas-Pennant. His flagship was the BULOLO. It was to be in his area that *Mulberry "B"* was to be constructed. The primary force landing on *Gold* was the 50th "Northumbrian" Division, commanded by Major General D.A.H. Graham.

The commander of the Canadian assault at *Juno* beach was Royal Navy Commodore Geoffery N. Oliver. Oliver was to bear responsibility for the *Gooseberry 4* of the *Mulberry*. His previous wartime experience had included command of the cruiser HERMIONE in the Mediterranean. After being promoted to the rank of Commodore, he had served as a special assistant to the Royal Navy's Flag Officer, North Atlantic Station. He had been at that post during *"Operation Torch"*, the invasion of North Africa in November of 1942. Later, during *"Operation Avalanche"*, the invasion of Italy at Salerno, he had commanded what was designated the "Northern Attack Force". In an interesting sidelight, the commander of the "Southern Attack Force" during that action was USN Admiral John Hall. This was the same Hall who was now serving as commander of the assault force off *Omaha* beach.

Oliver's flagship off *Juno* during the Normandy invasion was HMS HILARY. She departed Portsmouth at 1725 on the evening of the 5th. Also, aboard HILARY was British General Crocker, commander of 1st Corps, and Major General R.F.L. Keller, commander of the Canadian 3rd Infantry Division. Keller's unit was the primary unit making the *Juno* landing.

The Canadian forces landing on *Juno* beach were to have the weakest bombardment force supporting them. After reviewing intelligence reports on the German defenses in the area, two Royal Navy cruisers, the BELFAST and the DIADEM had been deemed sufficient for the task.

The commander of British assault at *Sword* beach, the most easterly of the Allied assault landing sites, was Royal Navy Rear Admiral Arthur G. Talbot. His flagship was the HMS LARGS (formerly the French liner CHARLES PLUMIER). His part of *Mulberry* was to be known as *Gooseberry 5*. The British 3rd Division, commanded by Major General R.G. Rennie would land on *Sword*.

Back at *Gold* beach, we begin to encounter the divided command problems that the British had saddled their *Mulberry "B"* with. The harbor construction there was to be commanded jointly by Royal Navy Captain C.H. Petrie and Royal Engineer Brigadier A.E.M Walter of the Army. Petrie was a hydrographer and Walter had served on the staff charged with evacuation from Dunkirk in 1940. Disagreements over responsibilities and procedures between the two would begin almost immediately. This naturally led to additional delays in the program's completion.

Due to the failure to maintain their construction schedule, and in fact falling far behind the fast-building Americans off *Omaha*, Petrie was later replaced by Captain Harold Hickling as naval officer in charge of *Mulberry "B"*. Hickling had been serving as Chief of Staff to RAM/P (Rear Admiral *Mulberry/PLUTO*) Admiral Tennant who was overall commander of the *Mulberry* operation.

Hickling had been involved in *Mulberry* since the beginning. He had a reputation as a rather brash New Zealander who didn't mind voicing his opinion on any number of subjects. From various statements he made after the war, he would probably have preferred a different assignment.

The failure of the British high command to have previously resolved the problems that such a command arrangement inevitably would cause, is almost inexplicable. Why someone in position of authority couldn't make the decision that the entire operation would be commanded by either the Navy or the Army is inexcusable. Why they chose to divide the command responsibilities between the two is a question that might better be answered by someone more familiar with the workings of the British military.

Again, in line with the policy of divided responsibilities, the actual assembly was to be completed by the Army's No.1 Port Construction and Repair Group. This unit was under the command of Lieutenant-Colonel Stuart Gilbert. Gilbert had been serving in the Mediterranean until February 1944 when he had received orders bringing him back to Britain. When he arrived, he was informed that he was to organize and train a special unit for a special operation in a matter of 4 months.

He requested that his former unit in Naples, Italy be transferred to Britain in mass to form a core group for his new organization. His request was granted, but he was told that he would have to count on transfers from other engineering companies to supply the bulk of his troops.

As has happened throughout military history, when a commanding officer receives an order to send a number of his command to another unit, he will naturally send his most expendable, and often his most troublesome, men first. And that is exactly what happened in this case. By the time D-Day arrived these unwanted undesirables had set fire to part of their camp and many of them were awaiting courts-martial. Fortunately, as also sometimes happens, these misfits would later perform their duties while under fire in an outstanding fashion.

The man actually in charge of assembling the floating roadways was Lieutenant Colonel Raymond Mais. Although he lacked the engineering experience of the type that might be looked for in a person commanding such a unique project, he was considered by his superiors to be a man that could adapt to different situations and would accomplish his assigned mission. After the war he would serve as Lord Mayor of London.

Unlike the Americans off *Omaha*, the British would not build their harbor directly off an assault beach. The town of Arromanches was actually slightly to the west of the British *Gold* beach. This meant that the first of the *Mulberry* *"B"* engineers would have to land on *Gold* and walk to their assigned area where they would then organize the assembly and layout of *"B"*.

According to the plan for the *Mulberry* operations, *Mulberry "B"* was to unload 7,000 tons of supplies per day. This was compared to the goal of 5,000 tons set for the Americans *Mulberry "A"*. This disparity was in large part due to the variations in the layouts for the harbors chosen by the two forces. These differences arose because of the various priorities given to the question of supplies versus troops and vehicles. The Americans preferred a harbor that would facilitate the landing of more vehicles and troops, while the British wanted more supplies ashore.

When viewed from overhead the British harbor appeared much more complicated and complete than the American. It resembled an actual harbor. The design for "B" called for four piers compared to the three the Americans would construct off *Omaha*. It was also enclosed at either end, while the Americans had chosen to leave the flanks of their facility largely open to facilitate access. It seems obvious that when the two layouts are compared that the British design would be much more effective as a shipping port while the American's would provide more protected beaches for landing craft to actually land directly on shore, which would have been their preference in any case.

The afternoon of June 7th saw the arrival of the first *Corncob* blockships that would form the *Gooseberries* off the three British/Canadian beaches. The officer responsible for building *Gooseberry 3* off *Gold* beach was Royal Navy Lieutenant Commander A.M.D. Lampen. Supervising Lampen during that operation was RN Captain John Jellett.

After modifying the original layout of *Gooseberry 3*, they decided that the steamer ALYNBANK would be the first ship to be scuttled. Unfortunately, during her placement, the tugs lost control of her and she sank out of position. Later three *Phoenix* caissons would be used to fill the gap that was created. On the plus side, this misfortune ended up adding an additional 110 acres of sheltered water within the harbor.

As the scuttling process began, it was realized that the ships would have to overlap one another to be effective. If there were any gaps left in the line, the actions of the sea would eventually scour or dig out the sand around the bottom of the ships. This would often result in the vessel settling into the newly created hole and breaking its keel. This would render it almost useless as any sort of defense against the waves of the English Channel. The last of the *Corncobs* wouldn't be emplaced off the British beaches until June 13th.

By the evening of the 7th more than 100 LSTs were anchored off-shore waiting to unload their cargos onto the British beaches. In order to alleviate this backlog, Admiral Vian stepped in and ordered the LSTs to be beached and dried out. Prior to this, the consensus among the British had been that stranding the vessels would result in damaging their bottoms. The operation went off without a hitch and by the afternoon of the 8th the congestion had been relieved. This solution was eventually adopted off the American beaches as well.

The reason for the logjam off the British beaches was the same as off the American beaches. The Navies had one set of priorities for which ships to unload first and the Armies had another. The Army wanted specific cargo unloaded, while the Navy insisted on unloading the first available ship. Eventually the Navy's preference was chosen due to the fact that with the confused conditions off-shore it was extremely difficult and time consuming to identify specific ships and ascertain their cargos. It was much easier and quicker to simply take the next ship in line, unload her and get her headed back to Britain for another shipment.

When the *Mulberry* tows consisting of the LST and stores piers began to arrive off Arromanches it was found that approximately 40% had been lost in transit. These losses were mainly due to improper towing procedures, inclement weather conditions and the inherent flaws in the construction of the concrete *Beetle* pontoons.

Mulberry components arriving ff the British beaches

The problem with the roadway tows was so severe that on the 13th Rear Admiral Tennant ordered that the size of those units being towed would be decreased from four 80-foot sections to three. This was done in the hope that the tows would be more manageable and that the strain on the *Beetles* themselves would be lessened.

When the placing of the *Phoenixes* at "B" began on the 10th, the building of "B" was already behind schedule. According to the *Neptune-Overlord* plan, by this date 6,000 tons of supplies a day should have been passing through the British *Mulberry* and it wasn't even operating yet.

It wouldn't be until the 14th that a stores pier would finally been laid to a length of ¾ of a mile. A Lobnitz pier-head was attached and the movement of vehicles across it began at once. A second stores pier would not be operational until the 7th of July. The completion of the second pier was critical to the proper operation of the *Mulberry* system. The piers were to be connected at their seaward ends and a circular traffic flow made possible. This would result in a much more efficient unloading process.

Soon after the first vehicle had crossed the completed first pier it was discovered that some of the pontoons for the floating roadways were out of position. This caused severe and unexpected stability problems whenever heavier loads were in transit. Fortunately, this problem was rectified before the completion of the entire installation.

The British get their first pier operational

By the 18th, the British had finished what they called the detached mole. This was one of many elements that were unique to the British facility. It consisted of 25 *Phoenixes*. It was designed to provide additional protection against the prevailing winds in the area.

In the first two weeks after their initial openings, the two harbors discharged just over 27,500 tons of materiel. While that was well below the projected total, it must be taken into consideration that most of that period was occupied by the storm of the 19th and the recovery from same.

In a somewhat related incident, the night of the 14th saw Royal Air Force bombers in action against the harbor at Le Havre. German naval units stationed there had been staging near nightly raids on Allied vessels off the British beaches. These had severely disrupted the construction schedule of the harbor as well as its use after completion. The air attack itself destroyed the large torpedo boats FALKE, JAGUAR and MOWE and 10 S-boats (smaller motor torpedo boats), as well as 25 R-boat (minelayers). This action all but eliminated the danger of German naval activity in the area.

Although the raid had greatly reduced the threat to Allied vessels off the invasion beaches, there was a downside to the exercise. The largely indiscriminate bombing which was a natural byproduct of bombing in limited visual conditions, had destroyed not only the German vessels within the harbor, but much of the harbor itself. When the Allies later took possession of Le Havre, they found that much of the damage they had to repair had been inflicted by their own forces.

The next night, the German naval base at Boulogne, further up the coast, received the same sort of attention. This time the count was 25 R-boats and several smaller craft. This action virtually ended any surface threat the German Navy might have organized against the invasion forces.

Seven miles east of Arromanches, and thus seven miles closer to the German forces at Le Havre, was *Gooseberry 4*. This facility was placed off the small fishing village of Courseulles located on *Juno* beach. During assembly, the engineers had received an unexpected surprise. It had been found that an uncharted reef off-shore would provide additional protection to small craft in the area. This, when combined with the fact that Courseulles harbor had been undamaged in the pre-invasion bombardment, afforded a most effective anchorage for Allied shipping.

This was very fortunate in that the fifth and final *Gooseberry* would turn out to be the least effective of all the installations. *Gooseberry 5's* problems, placed off Ouistreham on *Sword* beach, were not the fault of the crews assigned to constructing it. They had performed their duties as assigned. The trouble began German observers ashore sighted three naval vessels positioned just off-shore. They naturally assumed that a major operation was to take place at that locale. What they couldn't know was that the mighty naval task force which had so alarmed them was in reality no such thing. The three "warships" were in fact obsolete vessels destined to be part of the 9-ship breakwater to be built there. They were the Dutch cruiser SUMATRA, the British cruiser DURBAN and the French battleship COURBET. Naturally the German observers assumed that this was an active naval force that posed a threat to their defenses and so proceeded to do their best to neutralize it. The intense artillery fire that they directed at the installation soon rendered the *Gooseberry* useless as an unloading facility. Most of the traffic that had been destined for Ouistreham's *Gooseberry 5* was rerouted to *Gooseberry 4* off Courseulles.

During the storm of the 19th, the block-ships of the *Gooseberries* had fared much better than had been expected. While at *Mulberry "B"* priority had been given to saving the stores pier as it was nearest to completion. The effort was in large part successful, but the pier was still badly damaged and would require many repairs. The damage was such that the two *Spud* pier-heads were completely isolated from the shore. The half-finished and thus more vulnerable LST pier ended up suffering the brunt of the damage inflicted on *"B"* by the storm.

The *Phoenix* breakwaters were also to sustain major injury during the storm. Waves had begun to break over their tops soon after the tempest had started. This had led to severe flooding of the interiors. The thin concrete walls of the *Phoenixes* were designed to hold a certain amount of water in needed to secure them to the sea floor. But when the quantity of liquid within those fragile walls far exceeded the design limits. They began to fail when the tides receded, exposing them to unexpected stresses.

During the storm the *Bombardons* located further off-shore broke free from their moorings just as they had done off *Omaha*. They soon began to drift in towards the anchorages. Only alert and courageous work by the tugboat crews off the British beach succeeded in harnessing these runaways, thus preventing the damage incurred by the American installation.

When repairs on *"B"* eventually began, it was decided not to replace the troublesome *Bombardons*. Not too surprisingly, a later investigation by the British Admiralty found that faulty bolt connections installed during construction, rather than the inefficient and incorrect mooring procedures that had been used by the Royal Navy, were to blame for the design's failure during the storm. The same conclusion had been reached off *Omaha*.

Between the two *Mulberry* beaches more than 250 small craft were sunk or damaged when they were hurled onto the beach during the storm. Although many of those were later salvaged and repaired, most were scrapped where they came to rest.

The material which was eventually salvaged from the damaged American *Mulberry "A"* and sent to *Mulberry "B"* was used to repair and finish the LST pier. This was accomplished by the 17th of July. The landing of vehicles over that unit began immediately.

New, better built *Phoenixes* were eventually towed over from Britain and used to reinforce the original line of breakwaters. The newer units had covered tops to prevent their being flooded by high waves. The older caissons with their open tops were filled with sand to make them more stable and durable.

Mulberry "B" would eventually be nicknamed Port Winston in honor of the British Prime Minister. It would operate until November 19th although it had only been expected to last until September. It would handle a total of 615,000 tons of supplies. This comprised approximately 35% of the 1,817,000 tons landed by the British between the middle of

June and October 31st. An additional 13,120 tons of American supplies had also been handled by *Mulberry "B"* during this time period.

Until July 24th *"B"* was used mainly as a supply port with just over 2,000 troops being landed in the harbor. But, between the 24th and the operational end of the harbor at the end of October it would handle almost 25% of the 964,703 British troops landed during that time. It would also unload almost 40,000 of the 236,358 British vehicles landed in France between July 17th and October 31st.

The dismantling of *Mulberry "B"* began around Christmas of 1944. The first parts to be removed were the pier-heads. The piers were broken down with many of the sections being used to replace destroyed bridges in France, Belgium and Holland. A few of the *Phoenixes* were raised and used to fill gaps in the dikes at Walcheren Island on the approaches to the port of Antwerp in Belgium.

THE D-DAY LANDINGS

Before any landings could be attempted, with or without *Mulberry*, information had to be gathered. It wasn't just the German defenses that were of concern. The Allies obviously needed to know the water depths and tidal conditions that existed on the invasion beaches chosen for their amphibious landings. Another question often overlooked concerned the soil composition of the beaches. It had to be determined if the ground off-shore could support the weight of trucks and tanks. Conversely, the landing craft bringing those vehicles ashore could ruin their bottoms if it proved too rocky.

There were a multitude of facts and figures that had to be collected prior to the landings. At times, it almost seemed that information about the German defenses was secondary. In truth it probably was. If the invasion force was stuck in the mud off-shore, then the location and strength of the German fortifications would be the least of its problems.

As early as New Year's Eve 1943 the Allies had begun collecting intelligence on the prospective landing beaches. That night, a unit of British Royal Engineers commanded by Major Logan Scott Bowden, had swum onto the beach near Luc-sur-Mer. They took soil samples and gathered information on water depths. Most of their work was done below the tide mark to reduce the chances of detection by the Germans. A month later they performed the same mission near Port-en-Bessin and Vierville and a few weeks later did the same off what would later be called "*Omaha*" beach. The information gathered was used to determine the suitability of the various beaches for a landing. It was also instrumental in building scale models of the proposed assault beaches. These were kept in the two most secure locations in all of Britain, the War Department's Room 474 at the Metropole Hotel and in Churchill's War Cabinet Offices.

When the British commandoes returned with the news that the average gradient of the beach slope was only 1 foot for every 190 feet of distance, it definitely complicated the situation for the planners. It had long been realized that the extreme tidal conditions (a 20-foot differential) that were present in the English Channel would have to be taken into account wherever the landings took place. The shallow beach slope that was present off Normandy would restrict the possible options for H-Hour (the hour of the landings) even more than had been previously thought.

If it took place at low tide, the assault troops would be exposed the German defensive fire for an inordinate amount of time. If they went at high tide, there was the strong likelihood that their landing craft would become stranded as the water receded. This would remove the boats from operations for 12 hours until the next high tide. This presented a situation that, considering the shortage of landing craft, could never be tolerated. To lose the services of even a few could place the entire operation in jeopardy.

Intelligence was also needed concerning the topography beyond the high-water mark. Aerial photography could only show so much. The planners had to know what the assault troops were going to be looking at as they left their landing craft and began the journey to dry land and beyond. As a preliminary step, the British government issued a nationwide appeal to the public for photographs and postcards of the entire French coast, not just Normandy. This precaution was taken so as to alleviate any possible suspicions concerning the actual invasion location.

A seemingly innocent souvenir from a pre-war excursion across the Channel might reveal any number of important details, a potential exit from a beach, a possible location for a German defensive position, the gradient of a beach. These were items that would be vitally important to any future planning. They also might make the difference of life or death for the individual assault troops. The Allies could not afford to leave any stone unturned in their efforts to insure success in the upcoming attack.

Another critical source of intelligence was the aforementioned aerial reconnaissance. These flights were flown sometimes just feet above the waves, often directly in front of the German positions. For the most part, the aircraft involved were unarmed single-engine fighter planes that had been equipped with special cameras. Their only defense was their speed and the element of surprise. These courageous and largely forgotten pilots would provide priceless information on how the Germans were preparing to repulse the upcoming invasion. The photographs they took would enable the Allied High Command to plan the assault so that potential problems could be avoided or dealt with, everything from anti-boat obstacles in the water to defensive positions far inland. Every detail had to examined and re-examined.

Some of the photographs that were taken on May 1st revealed that there had been a major increase in the number of anti-boat obstacles being built by the Germans on the invasion beaches, especially the American *Omaha*. At first there was concern that the enemy might have secured information concerning the Allies' interest in the area. But, after much debate, it was decided that it was just a normal reinforcement of a potential invasion location. Post-war interrogations of German survivors would reveal that often when situations such as this arose; it was often just the result of an extra diligent local commander and nothing more.

Another major part of Allied pre-invasion strategy was called the Transportation Plan. It was a somewhat controversial series of attacks by the tactical and strategic Air Forces of the Allies that was intended to cut off supplies and reinforcements destined for the German forces on the Channel coast. Supreme Headquarters Allied Expeditionary Force (SHAEF) considered this action vital to the success of *Overlord*. Churchill and the commanders of both the Allied Strategic Air Forces strongly disagreed with that assessment.

Churchill's issues with the program were in the main, political. He and his advisors felt that the number of French civilian casualties might be prohibitive and could adversely affect relations with France after the war. But when the Free French Forces, commanded by General Charles de Gaulle, were consulted concerning possible civilian losses, they replied rather philosophically that it was war and people died in war. Victory was all that counted. Even after this reassurance, Churchill was still not convinced. He would eventually ask President Roosevelt to intervene, and order Eisenhower to reconsider the operation.

The issues with the strategic air force commanders were more military in nature. Although both naturally wanted to be involved in such an historic event as D-Day they preferred to do it in their own way. Air Chief Marshal Sir Arthur "Bomber" Harris, commander of the Royal Air Force's Bomber Command, felt his continued attacks on the German cities would eventually destroy German morale and force the German government to surrender, even without an invasion. USAAF General Carl "Tooey" Spaatz, commander of the American 8th Air Force, was of the opinion that his mass assaults on the German oil industry would be more effective in preventing German action against the invasion than attacks on individual rail-yards and bridges closer to the battlefield.

Eisenhower decided that he didn't have the time to wait for plans that might eventually have an adverse effect on the German defenders of Normandy. There were only 3 months until the invasion. He felt that a more direct approach was needed. He and his staff had determined that aerial attacks on targets that were more tactical than strategic in nature would be more effective and would make a bigger and timelier contribution to *Overlord*. He became so convinced that his direct control of the bombers was essential for success that he even threatened to resign as Supreme Commander if he didn't receive it. It was at this point that Churchill appealed directly to FDR for his assistance in changing Eisenhower's mind concerning the Transportation Plan. For one of the few times during the war, the President refused Churchill telling him that he would not contradict the on-site military commander in what that commander apparently considered the proper conduct of the war.

That had never been a problem for the rather meddlesome Churchill. He doubtless would have had some difficulty understanding the concept. He had an over-inflated opinion of his own abilities as a military strategist and never failed to inflict his theories upon his subordinates. Roosevelt, on the other hand fully realized that his abilities lay in the field of politics. He appreciated his own limitations when it came to military operations and was, in most cases, more than happy to leave the actual fighting of the war to his military commanders.

So, after much discussion, the Transportation Plan went into effect on April 17, 1944. By May 26th rail traffic between occupied Paris and the Channel was completely disrupted. The Germans attempted to alleviate this problem by trucking the needed supplies to their units on the coast. Unfortunately for the Germans, Allied control of the air over western France was so complete that even individual trucks weren't safe from aerial assault.

Even if the Allies hadn't reigned supreme in the air, the ability of the Germans to resupply their forces with the use of wheeled transport was severely limited. For despite having gained world renown as a highly mechanized organization, the German Wehrmacht didn't have a surplus of cargo trucks. Many of those they did have were in fact vehicles that had been captured from their vanquished enemies earlier in the war. For a modern Army, it was still extremely dependent upon the common horse for many of its transportation needs. And while fairly abundant and easy to maintain, horses were physically incapable of moving the thousands of tons of supplies needed by the garrison troops on the Channel.

The lack of wheeled transport that would afflict the German military throughout the war would at first seem to be incomprehensible in view of the availability of such automotive powerhouses as BMW, Mercedes, Porsche and others. The fault lay with the German military hierarchy. In their wisdom, they had decreed that those firms should focus their energies on building aircraft engines and tanks, the machines of war. If the Wehrmacht needed wheeled transport, it would just have to make do with what was left over after the production quotas for the war-making equipment were filled. The relatively few vehicles they ended up receiving would, by necessity be supplemented by the faithful horse and any enemy equipment they were fortunate enough to capture.

As for the political concerns about the Transportation Plan that had been expressed by Churchill and his advisors, they were fortunately proven wrong. There would indeed be civilian casualties during the campaign, but in nowhere near the numbers that had been feared. And after the war, those losses would cause far less discord in French-British relations than those suffered by the French Navy when it was attacked in North Africa by the Royal Navy after the French surrender in 1940.

Another matter which caused much discussion at SHAEF was the actual time the Allies would begin their landings. As mentioned earlier, the selection of this H-Hour, as it was known, was a bit more complicated than might be first thought.

The tides present in the English Channel were to cause major difficulties for the planners. The severe tidal fluctuations and the dimensions of the assault area meant that low tide at the western most beach, the American *Utah*, would occur more than one hour before the same tide at the last British beach to the to the east, *Sword*. The actual landings, as well as bombardment operations, would thus have to begin at *Utah* before those at the British beaches. This would serve to alert the German defenders and enable them to prepare for the British attack.

Everyone involved in the landings naturally had a preference for whatever time they felt would have been most beneficial to their specific operations. The engineers and demolition teams wanted low tide in the dark of night so they would have access to and time to destroy the anti-boat obstacles that barred access to the beaches. Darkness would also provide more protection against enemy fire. The Army assault forces wanted a high tide at night so that their troops would be exposed on the open beach for the shortest possible time. The Navy preferred a rising tide during daylight. Under those conditions there would be less danger of them stranding their landing craft than during a receding tide. It would also enable them to more easily identify the landmarks ashore that were critical to locating the proper assault beaches.

In the end, the decision was made to launch at dawn during a low tide rising. This compromise, as with most compromises, failed to please everyone. The Navy had the least reason to be displeased, while the engineers and demolition teams charged with eliminating the obstacles may have had the most.

The rising tide would limit the amount of time that the demolition teams would have complete their missions. If there were any unforeseen delays, they would not have sufficient time to destroy all the German obstacles before those obstructions disappeared beneath the surface of the rising tide. Also, in daylight they would be more exposed to intense German defensive fire. This was eventually proven by the losses they suffered on D-Day. The vital demolition teams, which were to have cleared lanes through the obstacles through which the landing craft of the assault waves were to have moved, were all but wiped out before they could complete their assignments. They would suffer the highest casualty rate of any of the units involved in the assault.

The demolition teams unlucky enough to be assigned to *Omaha* consisted of 272 men assigned to 16 individual groups. Each group was to have cleared its own path through the anti-invasion obstacles. Through no fault of their own they cleared just five before the assault troops began landing on top of them. These brave, conscientious and in many cases, doomed men were commanded by a naval reserve officer named Joseph H. Gibbons. By the end of D-day, 111 of Gibbon's men were dead or wounded.

This failure to clear the required access to the beach would result in the unnecessary loss of many valuable landing craft. It also caused a great deal of traffic congestion off-shore as the drivers of the surviving craft attempted to find a way through the obstacles and the wreckage that was accumulating at an alarming rate. But, most persevered and eventually made it to shore.

The story of the successful battle for "*bloody Omaha*" after they reached the beach is as well-known as it is oft-told. For that reason, we will leave the heroes of *Omaha* and move onto other aspects of the landings that might not be as legendary.

Each of the assault beaches had their own purposes and objectives, but the one that pertains most to our story was code-named "*Utah*" beach. For the American forces involved in that assault, their ultimate goal was the cutting of the base of the Contentin Peninsula and the capture of the port of Cherbourg at its northern tip. That harbor was critical to the buildup that was required for any hope of a breakout from the beach-head. Cherbourg had been the main reason that the American 1st Army Commander General Omar Bradley had insisted on landing the 4th Infantry Division on *Utah*, as well as the two American airborne divisions that were to land behind it.

The problems that the 4th Division had to deal with when it landed were far different than those of their compatriots in the 1st and 29th Divisions who landed at *Omaha* beach to the east. Whereas the terrain around *Omaha* rose sharply from the beach to form severe bluffs and cliffs behind and to the sides of the assault area, the topography of Utah consisted of your everyday sand dunes.

The issue for the forces at *Utah* was not what was directly behind the beach, but what was just beyond those gentle dunes. That part of the Contentin coast has large areas of salt marsh. Over the years the French had built roadways on man-made levees or causeways across those marshes to dry land on the other side. For the Allies, those raised roads would have to serve as exits from the confines of the beach. The depth of the water surrounding those causeways was normally just a few feet deep. It could be traversed by infantry. Vehicular traffic was another matter. That would be restricted to traveling along the elevated causeways, much like ducks in a shooting gallery.

If the Germans could maintain control of the landward ends of the causeways, even the infantry would be affected. They would be forced to wade across hundreds of yards of open area with the waist-deep water hampering them every step of the way. In a situation such as this, German fire could have inflicted casualties so severe that the Americans might have never gotten off the beach.

There were four these hypercritical exits which had to be seized by the invaders. The capture of their landward ends was entrusted to the paratroopers of the 101st Airborne Division. Obviously, American control of those points would have greatly reduced the amount of defensive fire available to the Germans to dispute crossings by the men of the 4th Division. Exit 1 was the southernmost and was at Pouppeville. Exit 2 came out at the village of Ste. Marie-du-Mont. Exit 3 led to

Audouville-la-Hubert after it crossed the flooded area behind the beach. It also passed within yards of the la Madeleine, the primary German strongpoint on *Utah* beach. Exit 4 terminated at the village St. Martin-de-Varreville.

The airborne troops would accomplish their mission, but as so often happened in airborne operations, not quite according to plan. Rather than the mass assaults envisioned by the planners, success was achieved through the heroic actions of small groups, or even individuals.

In what proved to be the last mass night drop for Allied paratroopers during the war, the men of the 101st were so badly scattered that in many cases it was to be several days before they could rejoin their individual units. It was up to each man as to how they reacted to their isolation. Fortunately, enough of them adapted to their unexpected circumstances and showed enough initiative to complete their missions. The total confusion that resulted from the night drop under heavy enemy fire and the fact that many of the aircrews of the transports were inexperienced and completely new to combat will be dealt with in more detail later in this section. Let it suffice to say that without the superb individual initiative and unit training of the paratroopers the story of D-Day on the Cotentin would have had a much different ending.

The inclusion of this airborne portion of the assault had been somewhat controversial amongst the members of the Allied High Command. Bradley had told Eisenhower that he would feel compelled to cancel the amphibious landings at *Utah* if he wasn't able to utilize the paratroopers to secure the territory behind beach. He felt that without the insurance of airborne support, the proposition was just too risky.

Ike also had to contend with the preferences of his boss, US Army Chief of Staff George Marshall. Marshall felt that dropping into an area more than 60 miles east of Caen near Evreux would be a more effective use of the airborne forces. He pointed out that there were already four operational airfields in that area. Those could be immediately put into use for the purpose of reinforcing the airborne troops. He was also of the opinion that an airborne strike further behind German lines would cause a more severe disruption among the German defenses.

After much soul-searching by the planners at SHAEF, it was decided that a more decisive use of the two American airborne divisions would be to land them in support of the forces landing on *Utah*. It was also feared that dropping them into the area recommended by Marshall would expose them to the very real possibility of being isolated by the Germans and annihilated.

Another issue that was a bit closer to home for Eisenhower than his disagreement with Marshall was the incessant doomsday forecast of his own Expeditionary Air Force commander, Royal Air Force Air Chief Marshal Trafford Leigh-Mallory. His constant and repeated message to Eisenhower was that the airborne divisions could suffer losses of 70% to 90% and that their operation should be cancelled. With the pressures of this huge undertaking weighing on his shoulders the last thing Eisenhower needed was for a subordinate to add to his concerns. In the event, the airborne losses were less than 20% during the actual landings. After the successful conclusion of the campaign, Leigh-Mallory would eventually send a letter apologizing for adding to Ike's burden.

Although no public record exists to confirm it, Leigh-Mallory was probably not the most ardent advocate of airborne operations. Later in the campaign, after several failed attempts by Commonwealth ground forces to take the city of Caen, Field Marshal Montgomery requested that the British 1st Airborne Division be dropped behind German lines to assist in the next attack. Leigh-Mallory refused, as he considered the operation too dangerous. He didn't seem to appreciate the fact that by their very nature airborne operations are always dangerous. But they were still a weapon available to be used.

Whether it was Leigh-Mallory's concerns about the operation or his own Eisenhower made a point of visiting the airborne troops on the eve of the invasion. He went to the airfield at Welford where the "Screaming Eagles" of the American 101st Airborne Division were waiting to depart for France. He personally visited with as many as possible and then waited as they took off. He then stood by the side of the runway and saluted each aircraft as it took off. Just after midnight, those paratroopers and many like them began landing on French soil.

The "devils in baggy pants" would be fighting and dying for hours before the men of the 4th Division began landing on *Utah*.

As with almost every other facet of *Neptune/Overlord* this operation had been planned down to the smallest detail and it had gone like clockwork until just before they were due to cross the French coast. That's when they encountered dense low hanging clouds that forced the C-47 pilots to spread out their formations. This had to be done in order to avoid the possibility of colliding with the all but invisible companion aircraft flying just off their wingtips. Unfortunately, when they finally broke out of the overcast they were scattered all over the sky.

As with most intricate and well-thought out plans, the one for the airborne assault on D-Day had become outdated almost as soon as the action began. No one knew where they were, not the pilots and certainly not the paratroopers riding in the back of their aircraft. Some aircraft conscientiously circled in mostly vain attempts to try and locate their assigned drop zones. Others simply hit the green light inside the aircraft's cabin. That was the signal for the paratroops inside to jump. As soon as they had disposed of their cargo, they headed for home. Several aircraft tragically dropped their loads into the sea where most of those unfortunate paratroopers were lost.

With the dispersion of the transport formations, there was virtually no hope of any unit cohesion once the paratroops had landed. They had in all likelihood been dropped miles from their assigned drop zones, in areas that were totally foreign to them. For months they had been studying their assignments and the surrounding terrain so that they could go directly to their targets and complete their missions. Now they were completely lost in enemy territory. They weren't even sure which direction to take to make contact with friendly forces, let alone find their assigned targets. And the men that were just lost were the lucky ones.

Large parts of the area assigned to the 82nd Airborne Division, which was dropped further inland than the 101st, had been intentionally flooded by the German defenders. Often the water was only a few feet deep, but when overloaded paratroopers dropped into it, many were drowned before they could even rise to their feet. On several occasions the only thing that saved many a drowning soldier was a sudden gust of wind that would catch his parachute and drag him to dry land. Once there he could then release his parachute and gather his wits to find that he was like almost everyone else, lost.

The same low cloud cover that had so disorganized the airborne operation on the Contentin would cause more problems behind *Omaha* beach. Heavy bombers of the American 8th Air Force were supposed to drop their bombs on the German beach defenses just prior to the landings. This would hopefully destroy those positions, as well as the anti-boat obstacles in the water. Additionally, the bomb craters would provide cover for the landing troops in the form of ready-made foxholes. Unfortunately, when the bombers arrived over their targets they couldn't see through the clouds. Rather than risk accidentally dropping on friendly forces, they delayed their drops for up to 30 seconds. In those few seconds they had flown 2 to 3 miles inland. When they finally did drop their thousands of tons of bombs, they probably killed more Norman cows than Germans.

The scattered aerial drop was a minor inconvenience for some of the paratroopers behind *Utah* and the kiss of death for others. At 0115 that morning, one "stick" (the group from one aircraft) of paratroopers from the 82nd Division was even more unlucky than most in their drop area. They landed right in the middle of the alerted German garrison of the village of St. Mere Eglise. The majority of those unfortunates were shot and killed before they could even release their parachutes and unsling their weapons.

Once on the ground the men of the 101st and the 82nd had two priorities. Find out where they were, and often more importantly to the individual paratrooper, find a friendly face. Alone in the dark in the middle of enemy territory even an independent minded paratrooper needed a buddy. It didn't matter whether the first guy they ran into was from their outfit or not, he was company and someone to cover their back. There were many instances of men spending days with battalions, regiments, even divisions that were not their own. Later they would often return to their own units only to find that they had been listed as missing-in-action, or even possibly killed-in-action.

Gradually, the troopers gathered into small groups. After a lonely night of wandering around by themselves in the dark, suspecting every shadow and jumping at every sound, the company of even a couple of men would have made the darkness of the night seem a little lighter.

If the chaotic dispersion of the American airborne troops had caused them no end of fear and frustration, it did benefit them in one way. It had totally confused the German High Command. They were receiving reports of paratroops from such a widespread area that they could not determine where the main Allied effort was being made. If the Americans had landed in concentrated groups as had been planned then the Germans could have at least made an attempt to confront them. As it was, as soon as they moved towards one reported paratroop position, another would be reported behind them. They were even more confused than the Americans.

At 0300 on the morning of D-Day, before the sun came up and while the paratroops were still trying to find one another, the first of the glider reinforcements began to arrive in the bocage of the Contentin.

The bocage was a maze of hedgerows that could stand as tall as 20 feet and were used by French farmers to separate individual fields. It was the polar opposite of the situation the British paratroops would encounter behind their beaches. Whereas the British often had an unobstructed view for miles, the Americans were lucky if they could see 100 yards. More often than not, it was far less.

The hedgerow system had been in existence since the time of the Romans. They almost resembled permanent structures. In many cases the hedges themselves had grown over the tops of many of the sunken roads that ran between the fields forming virtual tunnels through which the attacking Americans were forced to traverse.

The fields within the hedgerows were in the main far too small to land a fully loaded glider, especially at night. The men who had planned the operation had depended solely on aerial photographs to determine the landing zones for the gliders. For some unknown reason, no one thought to acquire local knowledge of the terrain. They had seen the hedgerows in the pictures, but had assumed that they were similar to the smaller hedges that covered the countryside of Britain. If they had been, then the gliders would have simply shoved their way through.

Sadly, for many of the men inside the gliders, the solid earthen banks upon which the hedgerows had grown were themselves often taller than the hoped-for British hedges. When a canvas-covered glider crashed into the embankment, it was like hitting a wall.

The hedges themselves were often so dense that a man could literally walk on top of them. Later in the campaign, these terrain features, which had seemed so insignificant in the aerial photographs, would play a major role in stalling the American efforts to breakout of Normandy.

The reinforcing gliders that came in that night were for the most part destroyed or heavily damaged and many of the supplies they were carrying were lost. The human toll was naturally the most crucial loss. Men that had been expected to reinforce and relieve the paratroopers, who had landed earlier, had to be rescued by those same paratroopers from the wreckage of their aircraft. These "reinforcements" became more of a burden than a relief to the men already on the ground. Among the many dead and injured was the Assistant Division Commander for the 101st Brigadier General Don F. Pratt, who was killed in the crash of his glider.

It was during this night of utter confusion that the training and adaptability of the American paratroopers came to the forefront. It wasn't so much the actions of the generals and colonels, it was the captains and lieutenants and sergeants, and in some cases the privates. They collected what men they could find, regardless of their assigned unit, and once they had figured out where they were, they set out to accomplish their missions.

The master plan had looked good on a map while they were sitting in a warm barracks in Britain, but now that plan wasn't worth the paper it was printed on. They had a job to do and the plan wasn't going to be of much help. They had to adapt to the new situation and do it on their own.

One of those missions for the men of the 101st was to secure the western ends of the causeways off *Utah* and that's where many of them headed. It didn't matter if they had 10 men or 110; they were going take those causeways, or die trying. An extra bit of incentive may have come from the fact that if they didn't secure those exits off the beach, the invasion could quite possibly fail. If that happened, there was no way out for the paratroopers. They were stuck. There would be no evacuation for them. It would be either a prisoner-of war camp or a grave in the Norman countryside.

As soon as these individuals had gathered what they hoped were sufficient forces to complete their missions, they headed for the coast. Often, they would continue to gain strength by collecting other paratroopers while en route to their objectives.

A prime example of this can-do attitude was 29-year old Lieutenant Colonel Robert G. Cole. He commanded the 3rd Battalion of the 502nd Regiment and was supposed to capture the village of St. Martin-de-Varreville at the end of Exit 4. He was also supposed to have landed near his objective with more than 300 men. What actually happened was that he landed almost 10 miles to the west of his objective with less than 30 men. After orienting himself, he headed east towards his target. By the time he reached it, his group had mushroomed to 75. This more than doubling of the size of his force apparently boosted his confidence, for after securing Exit 4; he split his force and sent part of it to attempt to capture the village of Audouville-la-Hubert at the end of Exit 3. Although the latter was not his assignment, he knew of its importance to the success of the invasion and realized the necessity of taking control of it if at all possible.

At 1300 that afternoon, Cole's men were on hand to greet the soldiers of the 1st Battalion, 8th Infantry Regiment of the 4th Division as they arrived at Audouville-la-Hubert from Utah beach. This was to be the first contact between units of the airborne and the seaborne assault. By the end of D-Day Cole's total force at the end of the two causeways had swollen to 250. This increase in strength was mainly due to the arrival of misdropped, but conscientious members of his battalion who had finally found their way to the coast. There were also several other units represented by men who had lost their way and had merely gravitated towards the largest group of Americans they could find.

It was at Cole's original objective, Exit 4 that one of the most remarkable and least known one-man actions of the war took place. The hero of this epoch is one Staff Sergeant Harrison Summers. Summers had been assigned by his battalion commander, Lieutenant Colonel Patrick Cassidy of the 1st/502nd, to take a German coastal artillery battery barracks behind the beach located in the village of Mersieres. It was to be known as WXYZ from its map coordinates.

Summers was assigned 15 paratroopers for the job, most of who weren't even from his own battalion. He didn't even have time to learn their names. When they arrived at their objective, the men assigned to the detail showed what could be considered understandable reluctance to follow this unknown sergeant into what appeared to be a potential suicide mission.

Hoping to lead by example, Sergeant Summers charged the first building and killed the four German soldiers that were in it. After coming to the realization that none of his men had followed him, he never the less attacked a second building in the group. After taking this one, he was gratified to see a single man of his group finally giving him some covering fire.

He then moved to a third house where he was joined by an airborne lieutenant who had stumbled onto the action. The lieutenant was badly wounded before they entered the building. Summers then charged through the door and killed six more Germans.

Almost in a state of shock Sergeant Summers knelt by the rear of his latest conquest and tried to collect himself. During this well-deserved break, he was joined by a captain from the 82nd Airborne Division. As soon as they stood up to attack the next building, the captain was shot through the heart.

Summers proceeded to take his next objective and killed six more Germans. At this point another member of his group finally chose to join him in the action. Together, they would take three more of the buildings in the complex and in the process would kill thirty more Germans.

There were still two more German-occupied structures in the area when his companion decided that he had had enough. In the second to last building Sergeant Summers, once again by himself, disposed of fifteen more of the enemy. When he reached the last and most heavily fortified of his targets, he was belatedly joined by the rest of his command.

During the following action, the structure caught fire. Thirty Germans who attempted to escape the flames were shot down. Fifty more would die and thirty-one would surrender before the area was completely secured.

In five hours of fighting, Sergeant Harrison Summers had almost single-handedly taken a position in an action that normally would have required a company numbering 150 men. He was awarded the Distinguished Service Cross and was commissioned as an officer for his incredible exploit. He had been recommended for the Medal of Honor, but the paperwork was lost. After his death in the late 1980's members of his group attempted to get it awarded posthumously, but failed.

To the south of Sergeant Summers' heroics, the capture of Exits 1 and 2 had been entrusted to the 506th Regiment commanded by Colonel Robert F. Sink. Within 2 hours of his landing in France, Sink had collected a grand total of 40 men. He was supposed to have nearly 900. He soon made contact with his 1st Battalion, commanded by Lieutenant Colonel William L. Turner. With the addition of Turner's men, Sink began to feel a little more like a regimental commander.

He then ordered Turner and his 50-man force (he was supposed to have had 300) to secure Exit 1 at Pouppeville. Being without the proper communications that are so vital to military operations, Sink assumed that his was the only organized force in the area. This situation led him to make the decision to split his small force in an attempt to take both important objectives. He couldn't have known that he was duplicating the efforts of another unit when he sent Turner south. It was just one more case of missing or damaged radios influencing the course of the battle.

Without the communication system they had grown accustomed to the Americans would spend most of this, their first day in France, fighting blind. They could only be sure of what was going on in their immediate area. There was no way to confirm that an objective had been taken or not. The most prudent action was then to assume that it had not and proceed accordingly.

The unit that was mirroring the assignment of Turner's battalion was the 3rd Battalion of the 501st Regiment. It was commanded by 28-year old Lieutenant Colonel Julian Ewell. He was advancing under orders from the division commander, Major General Maxwell Taylor. Taylor was operating under the same misconception as Sink. He assumed that his was the only force available to secure the critical exit, so he so he issued the proper orders for that situation.

It was now 0600, more than 4 hours since Taylor had landed in Normandy. For that entire period, he had been figuratively and literally in the dark. Since landing he had no idea where most of his major units were. This was to be his first decision worthy of his position as Division Commander that he was to make on D-Day. It was fortunate choice because Ewell's battalion ended up winning the unintentional race to Pouppeville and its Exit 1.

Although he had less than 200 under his command, he definitely enjoyed better odds than Turner would have had with his 50 men. For when Ewell arrived at his destination, he found it defended by 60 to 70 soldiers of the German 91st Infantry Division. The 91st was the closest thing to a first-rate division that the Germans had on the Contentin. It had been organized fairly recently, but had received specialized training in repulsing airborne attacks. Even with his numerical superiority, it would still take Turner more than three hours to secure the village. He would suffer 18 casualties in the action.

Ewell's force was waiting when a detachment of the 8th Regiment of the 4th Division crossed the causeway and entered the town. The group from the 4th Division was commanded by Captain George Mabry. Mabry would, as a Lieutenant Colonel, be awarded a Medal of Honor during the battle for the Huertgen Forest on November 20th.

While Ewell's fight for Exit 1 was still in progress, the 2nd Battalion of the 506th, commanded by Lieutenant Colonel Robert L. Strayer, was moving towards Exit 2 at St. Marie-du-Mont. Due to enemy resistance encountered en route, by the time they arrived at their destination they found that units of the 4th Division had already crossed the causeway and were passing through the town.

In an interesting sidelight, General Taylor's parachute jump on this night was just his fifth. He was now qualified to wear the paratrooper's wings on his uniform. Airborne trainees had to successfully complete 5 jumps before they qualified to wear jump wings and draw the extra $50 per month "jump pay".

Taylor's experiences earlier in the morning had taught him that a general's stars did not necessarily guarantee company on a night drop. After landing alone outside the village of Ste. Marie-du-Mont, he had spent more than 20 minutes looking for another American. He eventually crossed paths with a private from the 501st Regiment of his own division. Shortly thereafter he found his personal aide, Lieutenant Eugene Brierre. Within a couple of hours, he had collected a group that included 2 generals, 1 full colonel, 2 lieutenant colonels, 4 lieutenants, a few sergeants and maybe a dozen privates which led him to comment that "Never in the annals of warfare have so few been commanded by so many".

By mid-morning the men of the 101st had accomplished the first part of their mission, that of securing the inland approaches to the causeways. At the same time as those assigned to the causeways had been organizing their assault, other units of the 101st were heading south. They were to be responsible for securing the southern flank of the *Utah* beach-head and preventing German counter-attacks from the direction of Carentan. To do this they had to seize control of or destroy the bridges across the River Douve.

In what was an all too common occurrence on this confused night, a junior officer made a decision far beyond the normal responsibilities of his pay grade. Captain Charles Shettle of the 3rd Battalion, 506th Regiment had, like many others, landed far from his assigned drop zone. He had come to earth near the town of Angoville-au-Plain and soon had 2 lieutenants and 13 enlisted men under his command. Once he had oriented himself, he realized that he was closer to the objectives of the 501st Regiment than those of his own 506th. He elected not to wait to collect more men and immediately began moving towards the nearest objective that had been assigned to his division. His new destination was to be a pair of bridges over the Douve River at le Port. En route to his new target he did manage to acquire two more officers and 16 enlisted men.

When they arrived at the bridges at around 0430, they found 20 paratroopers from the 501st who had conscientiously moved towards their regiment's assigned objective on their own. After a conference with the other 9 officers in his small party it was decided to attempt to reach the far bank of the river and gain complete control of the crossings. They succeeded in this initial action and seized both bridges. After fighting off German counter-attacks for more than two hours, a lack of ammunition finally forced them back to the near bank.

Before making the decision to retreat back across the river, they had rigged the bridges with explosives. In the event that a further withdrawal was called for they could then set off the charges, destroy the bridges and prevent the Germans from crossing.

After being forced back across the river, Shettle came to the realization that he and his men had to have help. He had previously received word that a large part of the 501st Regiment was in position at the la Barquette locks. Those locks were located about a mile upstream from his position and had been another of the 501st assignments.

Shettle set out to make contact and hopefully procure some badly needed reinforcements. After arriving at la Barquette, he met with the 501st commander, Colonel Howard R. Johnson. He described the situation at the bridges and asked for some support. He was then informed that the Colonel couldn't spare any men or ammunition. He would just have to hold with what he had until he was relieved.

Disappointed, Shettle made the trip back to his men at the bridges. Having no other choice, they spent the rest of the day improving their defensive positions. Fortunately, the Germans across the river were apparently content with their lot and made no attempt to attack. During the day, another 40 stray paratroops wandered into American position. With these unexpected reinforcements, they were able to beat back a German counter-attack that occurred just before dusk. Throughout the night, more paratroopers would continue to stumble in, somewhat easing the situation.

The next morning, with his force numbering almost 150, Shettle began planning an assault to reclaim the other end of the bridges. Before he could move out, in what could well have been a scene from a Hollywood movie, United States Army Air Force P51 fighter-bombers swooped down from the sky and blew the bridges up.

Shettle's feelings as he sat there and watched the dust settle can only be imagined. After meeting with his fellow officers, the general consensus apparently, they had done enough. They hunkered down and stayed in their positions until they were relieved the next day.

Back at the la Barquette lock system Colonel Johnson and his command were in the process of securing their objective. Possession of the locks had grown in importance in the eyes of the planners back in Britain every time they had looked at them. The system theoretically controlled the water level of the Douve River well up into the Contentin Peninsula. Years before the war the French had constructed the locks so that they could stabilize the level of the Douve and provide more pasture land for the local farmers. Previously, the Douve had fluctuated with the rise and fall of the ocean tides. A high tide would force the waters of the river back upstream and out of its banks. When the tide receded, it basically took the river with it, and the riverbed became a mud flat. The construction of the locks had been the solution.

In November of 1942, more than two years after capturing the area, the Germans began constructing anti-invasion defenses along the coast. They decided to make use of this readymade defensive tool and use it to flood the Douve basin. Whenever an exceptionally high tide occurred, they opened the locks and allowed the river to flood the surrounding areas along the banks of the Douve as well as those of its tributary, the Merderet. They then closed the locks and prevented the water from returning to the sea. In some areas the inundated areas were up to a mile wide.

The way the *Overlord* planners had seen it, whichever side held the locks had Mother Nature on their side. They could use the river to open an avenue of advance for their own forces, or close it to those of their enemy. If the Americans controlled the locks, and the bridges that Captain Shettle was overlooking, they would be well on their way to securing their vulnerable southern flank.

The Germans apparently did not place as much importance on the locks as did the Americans. Their previous experience with the water level situation in the area probably had something to do with the relatively low priority given by them to the lock system. The small German garrison was overcome by the Americans after a short, but sharp engagement.

After securing the locks, Colonel Johnson finally began making preparations for moving 2,000 yards downstream to reinforce Shettle's force at the bridges. Before he could proceed though, the area came under intense artillery, mortar and small arms fire from nearby German forces. Fortunately, a naval shore fire control officer had been assigned to the 501st and it was at this time he began earning his pay. After making contact with the USN cruiser QUINCY, which was stationed off-shore for just this type of mission, he then directed that ship's 8" cannons onto the German positions. This resulted in the almost complete elimination of the troublesome fire.

Meanwhile the number of German infantry in the area around the locks began increasing. This caused Johnson to reconsider his previous decision to leave only a portion of his force, which totaled only about 250 men, to defend the position. He would remain with his entire unit. That way, he would have a better chance to maintain control of the locks which were his primary objective. Shettle would have to make do with what he had.

In yet another Allied military intelligence blunder, the locks were later found to be not as vital as they seemed. The levels of the waters controlled by the locks fluctuated so slowly as to be almost inconsequential in a fast-moving tactical situation.

Colonel Johnson was one of many in the two American airborne divisions that would survive the invasion of Normandy only to die during *"Operation Market/Garden"* in Holland three months later.

By the end of D-Day, the men of the 101st Airborne Division had reason to be satisfied with their initial performance during this historic event. Through a combination of tenacity and luck they had accomplished almost all of their goals. They had cleared the vital causeways for the seaborne forces and they had secured the beach-head's southern flank, although just barely.

Its sister division, the 82nd, had a different mission. The primary assignments for the 82nd were a bit different from those of the 101st. The capture of the small but important village of Ste. Mere Eglise was considered crucial. Control of it would cut the main road on the Contentin Peninsula, Route Nationale 13.

Route 13 ran from Cherbourg, down the Peninsula, through Carentan and on to the cities of Bayeux and Caen. It could serve as the main thoroughfare for any major German reinforcements attempting to reach the all-important harbor. Blocking it would also prevent German forces around Cherbourg from moving against the Americans during the early stages of the invasion.

The 82nd was also to destroy or secure various causeways over the flooded Douve and Merderet Rivers. This would help secure the southern and western flanks of the beachhead against potential German counter-attacks.

The paratroopers of the 507th and 508th Regiments of the 82nd were fated to suffer the worst air-drops of the entire operation. They were scattered over such a wide area that many men were out of contact with their division for 4 or 5 days. The lucky men amongst these orphans formed into groups. The unlucky ones, would do their fighting and dying alone. Both would fight many bloody skirmishes that would never make into the history books. Their fights were not always for specific military targets, but often just for personal survival.

Those two regiments were also to suffer the worst losses by drowning that night. As previously described, the Germans had flooded the area around the Merderet. Unfortunately, pre-invasion aerial photos had only shown what appeared to be a narrow river surrounded by a wide grassy expanse. For the paratroops the truth of the matter was sadly much different. The large meadow they were expecting was in actuality an area nearly a mile across that was covered in water from 4 to 5 feet deep. The fast-growing marsh grass in the area had acted as a perfect camouflage. One can only imagine the feelings of those men as they landed, expecting to come down on dry land and ending up sitting in water over their heads with more than 100 pounds of gear on their backs. Many of these unlucky men would end up just as dead as if they had been hit by a German bullet.

The men, who were fortunate enough to survive the tribulations of the swamp, gravitated towards a terrain feature that the planners had somehow overlooked. It was a railroad embankment that cut diagonally across the flooded area just north of the la Fiere causeway. It acted as a magnet for many of those lost and confused men who were wandering around in waters that were waist deep at best and over their heads at worst. As they moved to the only dry land they could see in the darkness, they also found the companionship they craved.

The Assistant Division Commander, Brigadier James Gavin, was one of those lucky enough to find this unexpected oasis. Once he was standing on an identifiable landmark, he was able to get his bearings and he began to organize an advance towards the division's assigned objectives.

Fortunately, as had happened with the 101st to the east, men of the two regiments would gradually form into makeshift units and would make vigorous efforts to fulfill their assignments. The primary of which was to secure the western ends of the causeways that crossed over the Merderet River. In moving towards their objectives though they began to encounter what was to be the bane of the Americans on the Contentin, the hedgerows. These hedges blocked not only the view of the surrounding area, but the sound of a friend or enemy that could be only yards away. They were so dense that often groups of paratroopers passed on opposite sides of hedges totally unaware that the comrades they so desperately sought were within a stone's throw.

The confusion and dispersion that resulted from their scattered landings had lessened the possible impact of these well-intentioned groups. Often after reaching their objectives, they found that they didn't have sufficient man-power to take them. In some cases, though, they found their targets on the western shores of Merderet to be almost undefended, the Germans having moved to east to the sound of firing in the direction of St. Mere Eglise. Even in those cases, commanders often found that they didn't have the men to properly secure what was theirs for the taking.

In contrast to its sister regiments to the west, the 505th enjoyed the best drop that night. It assignment was to capture the village of Ste. Mere Eglise, cut Route 13 which ran through it and to seize control of the eastern approaches to the Merderet causeways. Almost half of its members actually landed in their assigned drop zones, a rarity on this night. The majority of the rest were close enough to reach their assembly areas in a relatively short time. The 505th was thus able to rapidly move to capture Ste. Mere Eglise and secure the eastern causeways at la Fiere and Chef-du-Pont west of the town.

By 0430, it had occupied Ste. Mere Eglise and had established roadblocks to the north and south along the main road. They staged a small ceremony in the city center when they raised the same flag that had flown over Naples, Italy when they had taken that city the previous year.

As soon as the men of the 505th had taken the town they had begun to improve their defensive positions in order to deal with the expected German counter-attack. They didn't have long to wait. At 0930, a large force of Germans approached down Route 13 from the direction of Cherbourg. In the hard-fought battle that followed, the Americans managed to retain control of the town and the outlying roadblocks.

One of those roadblocks was located in the village of Neuville-au-Plain which was just north of Ste. Mere Eglise. One of the men killed in this action was a Sergeant Robert Niland. He was to be partly responsible for the plot of the movie "Saving Private Ryan". His brother Preston was to be killed the next day on *Utah* while serving with the 4th Division. Another brother, Eddy, was listed as missing in action in Burma the same week. The last of the 4 brothers, Fritz, was serving with the 101st Airborne Division at the time. When the chaplain for the 101st learned of the family's losses he attempted to have Fritz demobilized and returned to New York. Fritz refused and would serve on the front lines in Normandy until July 8th. His brother Eddy was eventually fund. As usual, Hollywood got just a little casual with the facts, but their business is entertainment and profit, not history.

By the end of D-Day the men of both airborne divisions had attained most of their objectives, but at a heavy cost. The 101st had secured the landward ends of the causeways off *Utah* and had established somewhat tenuous control of a portion of the southern flank of the beach-head. The 82nd had taken St. Mere Eglise, cutting the main north-south axis on the Contentin Peninsula. They had also established small bridgeheads on both sides of the Merderet River. Considering the nightmare that both units had jumped into the fact that they had accomplished this much, let alone even survived was almost more than could have been reasonably expected.

During the battle's post-mortem examination by the Allied High Command, it was decided that this was to be the last mass night-drop undertaken by Allied airborne forces. They had been extremely lucky to have succeeded, and at what cost? It would be weeks before the last paratrooper's body was recovered. Until the end of the war, it was to be daylight operations only for the Allied airborne forces. The last two major drops made by Allied airborne forces were *Operation Market/ Garden* in September 1944 and Montgomery's crossing of the Rhine in 1945. Both were accomplished in daylight.

Now we can move to the seaborne assault. This phase of the operation actually began at 0430 when 132 members of the 4th and 24th Cavalry Squadrons landed on the Iles St. Marcouf (a group of small islands) off *Utah* beach. It had been suspected that the islands were being used by the Germans as an observation post or possibly as a minefield control center. Neither of these were the case, but the islands were infested with anti-personnel mines which killed or wounded several members of the assault team.

At 0550, the Allied warships off-shore began their 40-minute pre-invasion bombardment. Minutes later 276 B26 "Marauders" of the American 9th Air Force began dropping 4,404 250 lbs. bombs on targets on and behind *Utah*. This action by the 9th Air Force proved to be one of the few really effective operations conducted by Allied bombers during D-Day. Among other things, it completely destroyed the German strongpoint at la Madeleine. This was the main German defensive position on *Utah* beach.

Almost everything up to this point had gone almost according to plan on *Utah*. But then the odds caught up with the Americans. The loss of some of the highly critical control vessels and a stronger than expected off-shore current in the area caused the entire assault force to veer off course. They ended up landing nearly 1 mile south of their assigned beaches. In the end this worked out well as the defenses behind the planned beaches were much stronger than those located behind the "new" ones.

Once they had landed and the mistake recognized, a decision had to be made. Either correct the error and send the following assault waves to the right beaches or bring everyone onto the beaches they were presently occupying. After a preliminary study of the terrain in the immediate area and the lack of serious German opposition nearby it was decided to adapt the original plan to their new location.

The most serious downside to this unexpected change in landing sites was that the plan had called for the use of specific exits for the movement off the beach. The soldiers in the assault waves had been trained to look for specific landmarks after reaching shore and when they didn't recognize the area they tended to wander around until they could ascertain their location. Additional time was also wasted in locating and clearing alternate routes through the seawall so that the forces on the beach could proceed inland. All this greatly added to the traffic congestion that would naturally have occurred even if the landing had gone according to plan. Caught between the rising tide and the 8 to 10-foot-high seawall the men and equipment of the 4th Division formed an almost solid mass that made German artillery fire far more effective than it normally would have been.

There has been some debate over who made this historic decision. The most likely candidate would seem to be Brigadier Theodore Roosevelt, Jr. He was the eldest son of the late President. He was also the over-aged Assistant Division Commander of the 4th Infantry Division with a bad heart who had begged and cajoled his way onto the initial assault wave. He was the senior officer on site so it would naturally have been his responsibility. He would die the next month of a heart attack and is buried in the cemetery behind *Omaha* beach. His actions on D-Day would result in his being awarded the Medal of Honor on September 28th, two months after his death.

Somewhat ironically, the Army had originally wanted to land at this specific location when preliminary planning for the invasion began. The Navy had refused saying that the beach gradient was too flat. The landing craft would come to ground too far from the protective sand dunes behind the beach. The Navy had been correct in their assertion that the distance would be greater, but the lack of serious defensive fire from the German defenders more than made up for the longer walk that had to be made by the assault troops.

Luckily, the number of casualties suffered during the landings at *Utah* beach would be relatively small when compared to the other assault beaches. The 4th Division suffered just 197 casualties during the operation and that included 60 men lost when their landing craft struck a mine well off shore. They had lost more men on their last training exercise *(Operation Tiger)* off Slapton Sands in Britain.

They still had their problems though. Until holes could be blown in the seawall, which ran the entire length of the beach, traffic congestion was to be a huge issue. The rising tide was shrinking the beach even as they watched. Succeeding waves of landing craft kept depositing their loads on an already overcrowded beach. Direct fire from the beach defenses was negligible, but long-range artillery fire from behind the beach was constantly falling into the landing area and would continue to do so for several days after D-Day.

Eventually gaps were blown in the seawall and vehicles could begin funneling off the beach. After breaching the seawall near Exits 1 and 2, the men of the 4th Division began working their way along the back of it towards Exits 3 and 4 to the north. They soon had all the causeways opened to traffic and began moving off the beach and towards their objectives for this first day of the invasion.

The men of the 4th Division would suffer from the same flaw in their training programs that afflicted many of their fellow soldiers in virtually every assault division on D-Day. So much emphasis had been placed on accomplishing the initial landings and then breaking through the German beach defenses that once these tasks had been accomplished, there was a tendency on the part of many to feel that they had done enough for one day.

Admittedly, the adrenalin rush that had carried them ashore had served its purpose and would probably have been replaced by a sense of relief and wonderment that they were still alive. They had fought their way through the thin crust of Hitler's vaunted "Atlantic Wall" and had survived. Most were completely exhausted, but the surviving German defenders were equally so. The more time the Germans had to recover, the tougher the next fight would be. If the landing forces had been trained to follow up their initial success and keep pushing their advance, they could in all likelihood have attained most, if not all of their D-Day objectives.

Even with the slower than hoped for progress by the 4th Division, it had succeeded in accomplishing several of its assignments by the end of the day. Sadly, one of the most important of those objectives had not been achieved. They were to have secured a designated landing area for a group of reinforcing gliders that were scheduled to arrive at 2200 that night. When the gliders arrived one hour early, they were greeted by heavy German ground fire. They were cut loose from their tow planes over what supposed to have been a secured landing zone. It wasn't, and many ended their flights by landing in what was still contested territory. Those that were lucky enough to land within the American lines ended up crashing into the ever-present hedgerows. As the injured survivors were pulled from the wreckage, it was again evident that once more the hoped-for glider reinforcements would prove to be more of a hindrance than a help.

For all their problems and mistakes, the American forces had established their foothold on the Contentin Peninsula. Their overall prospects for the future were brighter at the end of D-Day than they could have reasonably hoped for given the various misfortunes they had suffered. It had been a long day and there would be many more like it before they were finished with the fighting in Normandy. But they had won this first day and that gave them hope for the next.

The next day would be known in military parlance as D+1, one day after the landings. At *Utah* beach, the 12th and 22nd Regiments of the 4th Division would spend it strengthening their contacts with the airborne troops inland and eliminating the remaining German defenses along the coast. In the process, they had somewhat cautiously extended the beachhead two miles to the north. They were still far short of all their goals for D-Day, let alone D+1, but so was almost every other unit involved in the invasion.

These shortfalls were to force the first of many changes to the American assault plan. The 4th Division was originally to have turned north after crossing the Merderet River west of St. Mere Eglise. It was then to have taken the town of Valognes in its march towards Cherbourg. The recently arrived 90th Division was supposed to attack directly north out of the beachhead east of Montebourg and head for the same objective. Unfortunately for the American plan, the 4th Division was still hemmed into a far smaller beach-head than had been envisioned and it was nowhere near the Merderet River, let alone the town of Valognes. There just was not enough room for the 90th Division to maneuver as planned. General Lawton Collins, the VII Corps Commander, decided that the 4th Division would now attack northward out of the present beachhead as had been proposed for the 90th and take the towns of Montebourg and Quineville on the coast. Available units of the 82nd would attack north out of St. Mere Eglise on the left flank of the 4th Division, thus performing that unit's original mission. The 90th Division would have to cool its heels on the beach for a few more days while awaiting a new mission.

Another problem for the Americans had arisen on the beach itself. The supply issue that had been the sole reason for designing the *Mulberry* harbor in the first place, reared its ugly head soon after the initial landings. Confusion and congestion were the order of the day as hundreds of landing craft jockeyed for the scarce open spots on the beach. When one was unlucky, or unskillful enough to broach sideways in the surf, it naturally multiplied the problems, and this happened all too frequently. The unloading of the ships off-shore gradually fell further and further behind schedule. It eventually got to the point where

Admiral Moon, Commander of the Assault Force, considered delaying further convoys set to arrive from Britain. A decision of that sort would have had a snowball effect on the entire convoy system as schedules were reshuffled along the invasion front as well as back in Britain.

The overstressed Moon was also upset with the ship losses his force had suffered on D-Day. Although they had been relatively light, the casualties apparently weighed heavily upon him and he was seriously considering halting the unloading of supplies during the night. This could have been catastrophic for the forces ashore and the situation was deemed so critical that both Generals Bradley and Collins felt that they needed to maintain direct contact with the Admiral to prevent any other potentially disastrous decisions being made. Thus, at a point when the Army and Corps commanders at *Utah* beach should have been able to go ashore and acquire firsthand knowledge of the situation on the ground, they were tied to the flagship off-shore.

Brigadier General Williston B. Palmer, commander of the VII Corps artillery, finally persuaded Admiral Moon to allow the beaching of LSTs at the high tide. There they would remain to "dry out" until 12 hours later when the next high tide arrived. By the end of D+1 the Americans had landed a total of 32,000 men, 3,200 vehicles and 2,500 tons of supplies. The numbers sound impressive until it's realized that the plan had called for 39,722 men, 4,732 vehicles and 7,000 tons of supplies to be ashore by this time. Just two days in France and *Utah* beach was already far behind its supply requirements, as were its sister assault beaches further down the coast.

It was on D+1 off *Utah* that the Germans scored their most significant maritime success of the invasion. The SUSAN B. ANTHONY, one of the largest transports present during the operation, was sunk by a mine. Although personnel losses among the members of the 90th Division, who were aboard were not heavy, most of their equipment was lost. Mines were to be by far the greatest hazard faced by the Allies off the shores of Normandy during and after the landings.

The paratroopers, who had been fighting ashore since just after midnight of the previous day, had different issues to contend with. The 82nd still held tenuous control of the town of St. Mere Eglise and the critical crossing at la Fiere over the Merderet, but they still lacked communication with almost everyone. It wasn't until 0900 on the morning of D+1 that the division commander, General Matthew Ridgeway, was able to establish contact with VII Corps Headquarters, and then it was only partial. He knew he was transmitting, but he was unable to receive any confirmation from the intended recipients that the messages were getting through.

Eventually communications would be established between the paratroopers and the amphibious forces trying to reach them from the coast. It was just another case of the communications SNAFU (situation normal all fouled up) that that would hinder the Americans for days.

That same morning, the 82nd began sending out additional patrols to determine the situation in the surrounding area. One of them located a large enemy force that was sitting between St. Mere Eglise and the 8th Regiment of the 4th Division which was approaching from *Utah* beach. When another German formation was sighted north of St. Mere Eglise on Route 13, it was decided that the elimination of both would be the primary objectives for the day's operations.

The 8th Regiment to the south, assisted by a battalion of the 505th attacking from the north, would be responsible for the destroying the force situated to the southeast of the town. The rest of the 505th Regiment would strike to the north along the highway out of St. Mere Eglise and reduce the northern group. By the end of the day the action to the south had resulted in the killing or capturing more than 400 Germans and had secured the southern approaches to the town.

Before the remainder of the 505th could move towards its objective to the north, the intended target attacked them. The German armored force managed to reach the outskirts of the town before it was stopped. The presence of an American armored unit, which had fortunately arrived from the coast earlier, saved the day for the 505th.

Without the support of those tanks, the 82nd could well have lost control of the town, a possibility that could have had far reaching effects on the entire Contentin operation. The paratrooper units were not organically equipped with the weapons to deal with a large armored attack. That was a fact sometimes overlooked by the master planners.

After the morning's actions of D+1, things were beginning to look up for the Americans of the 82nd. The two main German threats to their position had been eliminated and they finally began to receive reinforcements by glider. The 325th Glider Infantry Regiment had landed between 0700 and 0900 near the village of les Forges, outside of Ste. Mere Eglise. They had suffered 160 casualties in the landings, but compared to the glider reinforcement attempts of the previous day, those losses were considered more than acceptable.

The 325th had originally been planned to act as a division reserve, but with the situation such as it was, its orders were changed to read that it was to advance directly into combat. It was to move to the banks of the Merderet and relieve the 1st Battalion of the 505th which had been fighting off German counter-attacks against the vital la Fiere causeway. The 1st Battalion would then be able to resupply and regroup for the next day's operations.

The conclusion of D+1 found the 82nd in a more secure position around St. Mere Eglise, but two of its three parachute regiments were still somewhat isolated west of the Merderet River. The division had still not accomplished all of its D-Day assignments.

Its sister unit, the 101st Division had been a bit more successful by the end of D+1. It had secured the beach causeways the previous day, could now focus its full attentions on reinforcing the southern flank of the beach-head. The focal point of that operation was to be the town of Carentan. It was at Carentan that the main road on the Contentin Peninsula, Route 13, made an abrupt turn to the east in the direction of Bayeux and Caen.

Their main attack would be down the road from Ste. Marie-du-Mont towards St. Come-du-Mont, which was less than 2 miles north of Carentan. There had to be a certain amount of urgency involved in the operation as the forces of Colonel Johnson and Captain Shettle were still hanging onto the la Barquette locks and the Douve bridges respectively. They had been surrounded by the Germans for the better part of two days and their positions might be lost if they were not relieved soon.

Unfortunately, that relief would have to wait until the next day at the earliest. The units of the 101st that were attacking from the north ran into unexpectedly heavy resistance during their advance towards St. Come-du-Mont. They were forced to stop for the night and consolidate their positions.

D+2 found elements of the 82nd and the 4th Divisions beginning to move north towards the German defenses based around the town of Montebourg. A good indication of how far the Americans were slipping behind their invasion schedule was that taking of Montebourg had been a D-Day objective for the 4th Division. It wouldn't be until D+7 that it was actually reached.

The next day, D+3, would hopefully mark for the 101st the beginning of the battle for Carentan and the complete security of the southern flank of the VII Corps area. Not only was the possession of Carentan vital for the protection of the American forces in the Contentin, it was the also the first link in the chain that would eventually consolidate the individual assault beaches into one continuous front.

At 0445, the 101st renewed its assault on the German defenses at St. Come-du-Mont. They eventually broke through and finally relieved the forces commanded by Colonel Johnson and Captain Shettle along the Douve River. They immediately regrouped and set out in the direction of their ultimate goal, the road junction at Carentan.

The plan for the taking of Carentan was to involve a pincer movement around the town. But, for the first time since landing the Americans would be fighting an entrenched, determined and organized German force. They were expecting a tough fight and they weren't going to be disappointed. The main attack was set to begin early on the morning of June 10th (D+4).

The attack to the right of the town would be spearheaded by the 3rd Battalion of the 502nd Regiment, commanded by Lieutenant Colonel Robert G. Cole. It was to be upon this portion of the assault force that much of the hardest fighting would fall.

A major problem for the 3rd Battalion was the fact that the only route of advance available to them was a single causeway that ran from the Douve River towards Carentan. The causeway stood 7 feet above the surrounding flooded area and gave the paratroopers the appearance of ducks in a shooting gallery as they tried to cross. As they began their advance, Cole was in the lead. Less than 150 yards from the end of the causeway, they were forced to the ground by German machinegun fire. Cole, after being pinned down for more than an hour by the German machineguns, had had enough. He drew his pistol and then led his men against the German positions in one of the few bayonet charges of World War II. After clearing the causeway, they were reinforced by the 1st Battalion commanded by Lieutenant Colonel Cassidy.

The end of the day found both battalions dug into defensive positions near the end of the causeway. The next day, June 11th was to be one of almost constant fighting as the Americans attempted to hold their positions. At 2000 that evening the two tired battalions were relieved by the 2nd Battalion of their own regiment. It was then decided that the 502nd had been so depleted by the fight for the causeway that it would be replaced for the final assault on Carentan by the 506th Regiment.

Cole was awarded the Medal of Honor for his actions that day outside of Carentan. Sadly, he was killed in action on September 19th during *Operation Market/Garden* in Holland before he could receive it.

On the left flank of the attack on Carentan, it was to be the 327th Glider Regiment carrying the initial load. On the morning of the 10th, it began crossing the Douve near the village of Brevands. In addition to attacking Carentan from the east, it was also to link-up with units of the V Corps which were approaching from *Omaha* beach even further to the east.

About a mile and a half outside of the village of Auville-sur-le-Vey, they encountered their first heavy German resistance. After a short, but sharp action, they entered the village and made contact with a patrol from the 29th Division of V Corps, which had arrived from the east. They then moved out towards their next objective, the town of Carentan.

By 2000, on the evening of the 11th, they were in position outside Carentan. They had accomplished their goal and would step aside the next day and watch elements of the 501st Parachute Regiment and the 401st Glider Infantry Regiment attack the town.

At 0200 that next morning, the Americans to the east and north began moving forward. By 0730, they had surrounded and gained control of the town. Unfortunately, the bulk of the German garrison had been allowed to escape the trap. They had slipped out to the south before the town was completely encircled.

Now that the 101st had taken the last of its primary invasion objectives, it began to further strengthen its positions defending the southern flank of the VII Corps area. It also needed to solidify its contact with the V Corps at *Omaha* beach. On the morning of the 13th as they were preparing to do just that, they were hit by a German counter-attack.

The Germans advanced to within 500 yards of the outskirts of Carentan before they were stopped. The situation was deemed serious enough that V Corps on *Omaha* beach withdrew some of its tanks from its own offensive operations and sent them to assist the 101st in repulsing the German assault. The arrival of those tanks turned the tide in favor of the Americans.

With this attack from a new and unexpected direction, the Germans decided that discretion was the better part of valor and began to withdraw. By 1030 that morning, those same tanks of the 2nd Armored Division rumbled into the middle of Carentan. The two American assault beaches were now solidly connected forming a continuous front capable of repelling all but the most powerful German counter-attacks.

The next day, on the 14th, the 82nd and 101st Divisions linked up at the village of Baupte to the west of Carentan. This closed the last gap in the frontlines of the American airborne forces. The American high command could finally breathe a little easier. They immediately began making plans for the conquest of the rest of the Contentin Peninsula.

At this point, after completing their assignments, the two airborne divisions were supposed to have been pulled out of the frontlines for rest and replenishment. The primary function of the airborne forces was to act as shock troops during initial attacks, after which they were theoretically to be withdrawn until those services were needed again. In most cases during the war however, it was usually determined by the local area commander that they couldn't be spared. This time was no different. Instead of returning to Britain to recover and retrain, both divisions were eventually transferred to the newly activated VIII Corps.

VIII Corps was to be responsible for the security of the southwestern flank of the VII Corps as it completed the conquest of the Contentin Peninsula.

General Omar Bradley, Commander of the US 1st Army, had on June 9th ordered that any further advance towards Cherbourg be considered secondary to gaining control of the base of the Contentin Peninsula. Now that VII Corps had become more comfortable with its tactical situation it could begin carrying out Bradley's directive. It was decided to move the until now inactive 90th Division through the 82nd Division's la Fiere bridgehead over the Merderet River. After crossing the river, it was to continue its advance towards the west coast of the Contentin and thus complete the isolation of Cherbourg from the rest of France.

While the 82nd Division was awaiting the arrival of the 90th, it was awarded its first Medal of Honor of the Normandy campaign. On June 9th a platoon from the 325th Glider Infantry Regiment of the 82nd attempted to expand the la Fiere bridgehead. In the process of which they were cut off by a superior German force. They had no hope of retreating to safety until Private First-Class Charles N. DeGlopper volunteered to give them covering fire. Taking his B.A.R. (**B**rowning **A**utomatic **R**ifle) he moved to the center of the road and began firing into the German positions. As he stood there, in full view of the Germans, he was hit repeatedly as he drew the fire away from his comrades. By the time he slumped to the ground dead, his platoon had safely withdrawn. For a variety of bureaucratic reasons, his citation for the Medal wasn't issued until February of 1946.

Soon after DeGlopper's heroics, lead units of the 90th Division began reaching the crossing. The 90th was also to assume responsibility for another causeway located at Chef-du-Pont to the south of la Fiere.

After three days the division had accomplished next to nothing. It was, for the most part, still occupying the same positions recently vacated by the 82nd without exhibiting sufficient offensive zeal in the opinion of the high command. The decision was made at VII Corps headquarters that they had waited long enough. A change was needed and it was needed quickly. Every day that the Contentin wasn't cut was another day the Germans could use to reinforce their garrison in Cherbourg. The division commander and two of his three regimental commanders were to be replaced.

This was not an uncommon occurrence within the American army during the war. There was such a surplus of senior officers available that there was little hesitation in relieving anyone which who not performing up to par. Often times those that had been displaced were given other assignments at which they excelled. Sometimes apparently all that was needed was a change of scenery.

The new leader of the 90th would be Major General Eugene Landrum. Landrum had previously been serving as Assistant VII Corps Commander. It was fervently hoped by his superiors that he would get the 90th operating as they thought it should. When Landrum assumed command, he was given instructions that he was to clean house and not hesitate in removing anyone, regardless of rank.

This he did, but to no avail. The performance of the 90th continued to be substandard and by July 30th Landrum was gone as well. During his short tenure, a battalion position had been lost and two full companies had surrendered to the enemy. The situation had reached the point where serious consideration was given by 1st Army Headquarters to disbanding the entire unit and utilizing its personnel as replacements for other units.

The salvation of the division's reputation, as well as possibly its actual survival, arrived in the person of its next commander, Brigadier General Raymond S. McLain. He immediately replaced 16 senior officers. He also set out to improve the morale and the training within the division. When he finally departed the following October to assume command of a corps, he left his replacement one of the best American divisions in the European Theater.

But, until McClain arrived to take charge, 90th Division offensive operations would continue to founder. The Contentin still had to be cut, if not by the 90th then by someone else. The VII Corps commander, General Lawton Collins, decided on June 12th that elements of the 82nd, along with the newly arrived 9th Division were to do the job. The 90th, although it had been relieved of its primary mission, could not be spared from front line duty. The decision was made to merely turn it to the north and have it protect the flank of the divisions that had taken over its place. Bradley had requested a replacement division, the 79th, but that unit was not yet ashore.

By June 15th enough American troops had been landed on *Utah* that 12th Army Group could activate another corps on the Contentin Peninsula. General Corlett's brand new XIX Corps would assume responsibility for the Carentan sector overlooking the town of St. Lo to the south.

On June 17th, units of the 9th Division finally reached the western shore at the coastal town of Barneville-sur-Mer. Now the process of completely sealing off the peninsula could begin as ordered. The 82nd Airborne had actually cut the last road north to Cherbourg the previous day, but the capture of Barneville-sur-Mer eliminated the possibility of any large German forces sneaking through.

The German high command meanwhile had its own problems. On June 14th, they finally saw the writing on the wall and had begun transferring what remained of their naval forces in Cherbourg to the ports of St. Malo and Le Havre. They had finally come to the realization that the loss of Cherbourg might be delayed, but it was not going to be prevented.

With the Allies firmly established in Normandy, it was well past time for the main German forces to retire to more defensible positions further within France. This was an opinion shared by most in the German high command. But, unfortunately for them, it was not up to them. In Nazi Germany, Hitler alone could make such important strategic decisions.

Field Marshal Erwin Rommel, the German area commander, had long realized that when the Americans gained control of the Contentin, the city of Cherbourg and its German garrison were as good as lost. Any counter-offensive that he might attempt in an effort to relieve the German forces defending the harbor was doomed to failure.

Even if he did succeed in breaking through the American defensive line to the south, the Contentin Peninsula was so narrow that Allied naval gunfire fired from either side of it could cover the entire land mass. He would be under constant artillery fire from which there was no escape. That same over-whelming firepower that could be delivered by the Allied warships off-shore was one of the main reasons the invasion had succeeded in maintaining a beach-head in the first place.

Prior to the invasion, Rommel had been warned by several senior German commanders, including one of Germany's leading experts on armored warfare, General Heinz Guderian, that naval gunfire would pose a major threat to his forces. He was advised that he should keep his armored units further inland where they would not be within the range of Allied warships. They could then stage the necessary counter-attacks without fear of the devastating fire. Those commanders had learned this deadly lesson during the campaigns in Sicily and Italy. There, the Allied naval gunfire had virtually destroyed every German attempt to attack the invading British and American forces.

He not only chose to ignore this advice, he threatened to dig in every tank under his command and make use of them as immobile pillboxes in his beach defense. Unlike the other German commanders, he had learned about war in North Africa. In that theater, the Allied control of the air had been his biggest concern, not naval bombardment.

In the main, his forces in North Africa were usually too far from the sea to have been seriously affected by naval gunfire. His experience in that theater had taught him that once the invasion started Allied aircraft would make any attempt to move forces forward almost suicidal. He wanted his units close to the beach where they would not have to risk any more movement than was absolutely necessary. If that rendered them all but immobile then so be it, at least they would be comparatively safe from air-attack.

He was also certain that he could expect no significant assistance from the German Air Force, the Luftwaffe. Years of fighting a defensive battle on the Western Front against the massive Allied bomber fleets, as well as the costly battles on the Eastern Front, had reduced the Luftwaffe to a shell of its former self. Most of the fighters that had remained in the west had been transferred back to Germany itself to defend the factories and cities of the Homeland. The few hundred German aircraft available for the defense of France would be totally overwhelmed by the thousands of Allied aircraft that filled the sky. There came to be a saying in the German Wehrmacht that if an aircraft overhead was blue it was British, if it was silver it was American and if it was invisible it was German.

The quandary for the German commanders charged with defending Normandy, was that they were caught in a no-win situation. Advocates of both strategies just knew they were right, but in actuality, neither option would have worked. After the invasion, every attempt by the Germans to bring fresh units forward resulted in those forces, if they arrived at all, showing up late and having been badly mauled by Allied airpower while en route.

Rommel, on the other hand, had learned the hard way just how devastatingly effective naval gunfire was. Until his forces had retreated beyond its range, even individual vehicles moved during daylight at their own peril. He would also find that the bulk of his vaunted fixed beach defensive positions were themselves almost defenseless. Most had succumbed after less than one day's resistance.

During the invasion, that Allied armada of firepower which had caused so much discord within the German High Command was almost immune to any attempts by the paltry German naval forces stationed along the English Channel to disrupt its operations. Allied shipping was so numerous and their defenses were so strong off the Normandy coast that they could easily afford the loss of the few vessels that the Germans managed to sink.

The closest thing to a major warship loss suffered by the Allies on D-Day to direct German naval action was the Norwegian destroyer SVENNER. She was sunk at 0537 hours off the British *Sword* beach by S-boats that ventured out from the port of Le Havre.

By far, the most successful naval operation conducted by the Germans had been the laying of thousands of anti-shipping mines off the coast. These would cause numerous ship losses for the Allies on D-Day and would continue to do so long after the Allied armies had moved inland.

After realizing the futility of trying to hold the Allied forces on the beach, Rommel had appealed directly to Hitler for permission to withdraw further inland. He had come to the inescapable conclusion that his only hope for survival lay in retreat. He had to move back to a point where he could concentrate his forces for the all-important counter-attack without interference by the fleet of Allied warships that cruised almost unhindered along the coast.

But Hitler, as almost always, refused to authorize retreat. Retreat was not an option available to German officers on any front of the war. Here on the Channel coast when first arriving to assume their commands, they had even been required to sign a document stating that they would never relinquish any ground to the enemy. This unimaginative and conservative policy of never giving up conquered territory had cost Hitler dearly on the Eastern Front and would continue do so in the West.

Rommel, knowing that the port of Cherbourg would eventually fall into Allied hands chose the only viable option available to him. In accordance with Hitler's wishes, he ordered the garrison to fight to the last bullet and the last man. He then contacted local commanders and directed them to use every means at their disposal to completely destroy the harbor and its facilities. He still did not fully appreciate the fact that *Mulberry* was to serve as a temporary supply port for the Allies. He felt that if he could deny them a supply base at Cherbourg, he could still starve them out and still win the battle of Normandy.

Another issue that was worrying Rommel was that he still was not completely convinced, even at this late date, that Normandy was the main objective of the Allies. During the first few critical days after the invasion, he would still take time to travel to the Pas de Calais to inspect its defenses. He wanted to make sure that the troops stationed there were alert and ready for the invasion that he felt was still coming.

Back on Normandy, where the real invasion was taking place, the Americans were beginning to feel more secure. With solid protection to the south of the beach-head, the VII Corps could finally put all their efforts into their attack north towards Cherbourg. The officers at Corps headquarters were more than a little concerned about the continued failure to attain their assigned objectives on schedule. If by some chance they forgot that they were falling behind, the staff at 1st Army was sure to remind them.

It could have been even worse for VII Corps if it hadn't been for the unwitting cooperation of the Germans. The Wehrmacht had built a reputation throughout the war of aggressively reacting to their opponent's movements. In this instance though, they were shackled by a bizarre command structure and the continued success of the deception plan *Operation Fortitude*. By the time they had figured out that the Allies main effort was actually in Normandy and not in the Pas de Calais and had made a decision on where to counter-attack, it was too late. By that time, the Allies were firmly established in France. They had also nearly completed the required build-up for their upcoming breakout from the beachhead.

A lack of training no doubt also contributed to the general lack of offensive spirit among the defenders. A common complaint made by German unit commanders in the coastal zone was that their men had spent more time building anti-invasion defenses than training for their primary function of repulsing an invasion. When Rommel had assumed command of the area in January, he had given the highest priority to construction rather than training.

Another factor in the lack of response by the Germans against the Allied beach-head was the quality of the individual soldiers serving along the coast. They were not the elite handpicked native Germans that had formed the core of the German Wehrmacht at the beginning of the war. That Wehrmacht no longer existed. The Soviets on the Eastern Front had all but destroyed it.

Many of those now serving in the "static" or defensive divisions that manned the Atlantic Wall defenses were "untermenschen" (or sub-human in German parlance). They were inhabitants of conquered territories in the east. There were captured Poles and Czechoslovakians and disenchanted Soviet soldiers fighting for their German masters. They had joined the German Army to fight communism or to escape the almost certain death of the prisoner of war camps. There were even Korean nationals who had been captured during the short-lived war between Russia and Japan in 1939.

Even many of the ethnic Germans serving in those units were considered by the German High Command to be of inferior quality. They were often referred to as "stomach battalions". That was Wehrmacht slang for men that had previously been considered as unfit for military service due to physical infirmities.

Once the Allies had landed, these somewhat less than devoted troops were often held in their positions by their German superiors who threatened to shoot them if they tried to surrender or retreat. They had been told since arriving in Normandy that even if the Allies did take them captive, they would be shot as traitors to the Allied cause. While men in this situation could be forced to man defensive positions, it would be all but impossible to force them to mount any sort of effective counter-attack. To paraphrase one German general, they were asking Russians to fight Americans in France for Germany. That was asking a lot.

Of all the "German" divisions holding the defenses along the Normandy coast on D-Day, only the 352nd could be considered first rate. The 91st Luftwaffen Division based in the Contentin, consisted of mainly Air Force personnel who were by and large new to the life of an infantryman, but at least they were physically fit Germans. Another decent division, the 77th, would make its way into the Contentin from its position in Brittany before the end of the battle, but would arrive so late as to have almost no real influence on the outcome.

THE TAKING OF CHERBOURG

After the temporary facilities of the *Mulberries* and *Gooseberries* had been completed, the Allies still needed to secure a real seaport. The Mulberry program was nothing more than a stopgap solution to the supply problem that confronted the invaders. That was a fact that even its most vocal proponents would freely admit.

The harbor at Cherbourg was to be the Americans primary objective. It and the city of Caen on the British front were considered to be the most important objectives to be taken as soon as possible after a successful landing.

When the original Cherbourg assault plan was laid down by the VII Corps headquarters back in Britain, it was decided that the 90th Infantry Division, commanded by Brigadier General Jay MacKelvie, was to have advanced on the 4th Division's right in the direction of Cherbourg within a couple days of the landings.

That plan didn't survive the first week of the Allied landings. The failure of the 4th Division to sufficiently expand the beach-head behind *Utah* beach, as well as the dismal showing of the 90th Division once it had landed, would lead to major modifications.

Eventually, MacKelvie was relieved of his command. He had been the division's artillery commander until just weeks before it left Britain for Normandy. When he was relieved, it was "without prejudice" in view of the short time in which he held command.

According to that same original plan, the 9th Infantry Division was to have served as the Corps reserve for the attack towards Cherbourg. After the early lack of progress by the 4th and 82nd Divisions and the less than satisfactory performance by the 90th, the mission of the 9th was changed. It was destined to become a major player in the story of the campaign on the Contentin.

After successfully cutting the base of the Contentin and securing his left flank against the possibility of a counter-attack by the German forces based in the heart of France, Bradley was finally free to take the bulk of his forces and head north for Cherbourg. He knew as well as anyone how important it was to his supply situation. He had to take it as soon as possible.

On the 18th, at a meeting between Bradley, Collins and several division commanders, it was decided that three divisions, the 4th the 9th and the newly arrived 79th, would attack north towards Cherbourg the next day. The 90th Division was still trying to live down its disappointing start and was apparently not yet considered ready for prime time. The commanders and staff of the American VII Corps had adapted, and had modified their operations to fit the situation at hand. They were well behind schedule, but they were at last moving in the right direction.

On the 19th, the demand to take the port of Cherbourg would become even more urgent. A major storm hit the coast and would last for 4 days. It would severely damage the *Mulberry* harbors and would almost completely disrupt the unloading operation over the beaches. Collins would use this fact to encourage his commanders to spare no effort in their upcoming offensive against the now even more critical seaport.

Opposing the American advance would be elements of four German divisions, the 243rd the 77th the 357th and the 91st. All had been involved in heavy fighting and had their ranks badly depleted.

The first, as well as the most important, objective of the American move towards Cherbourg was to gain control of the terrain between Quineville, La Pernelle and Montebourg. This area constituted the last major defendable position for the Germans before Cherbourg.

Of the three attacking American divisions, the 9th would face the most resistance. At 0300 on the 19th it began its attack and would come up against fairly formidable German defenses around the town of Montebourg. After breaking through a thin crust of defenders they were to have a relatively easy advance until they reached the outer defensive positions around Cherbourg. Two hours later the 79th and 9th Divisions began their attacks against even lighter opposition.

Almost as soon as the American offensive began on the 19th, the senior German commander on the Contentin, General Karl Wilhelm von Schlieben, decided to withdraw his main forces inside the Cherbourg defenses. The rearward movement of the German formations began that evening. They were so fatigued and disorganized that almost no rear-guard actions were fought to slow the American advance.

The evening of the 19th saw VII Corps headquarters issue orders for the objectives of the next day. The 9th Division on the left flank was to advance to the west of Cherbourg and cut it off from any possibility of reinforcement from Cap de la Hague. The 79th, in the middle would move towards the western suburbs of the city and begin probing the German defenses. The 4th would be responsible for isolating Cherbourg from the east.

The action that the Americans would face on the 20th would make them appreciate the relatively easy time they had enjoyed the day before. The terrain of the Contentin in the north around Cherbourg is much hillier than that in the south and was more open due to the lack of the bocage. This fact, when combined with the increased resistance from the German forces which were being compressed into a smaller and thus more easily defended area, was going to call for a change in tactics previously used by the Americans. Whereas they had been able to outflank many German defensive positions unobserved in the hedgerow country, they were now forced to take a more direct approach in their assaults.

Although the Americans attained most of their objectives by the end of the 20th, they weren't where they had hoped to be. They were again falling further behind schedule. That night was spent probing the German defenses in an attempt to find a weakness that they could exploit the next day.

The 9th and 79th Divisions spent most of the 21st basically treading water and sending out patrols much as they had the previous night. They needed to further establish the locations of the Germans and to formulate a plan for next day's activities. The 4th, on the right flank encountered less resistance and was able to make some limited advances towards the rest of their previous day's objectives.

By that evening General Collins felt justified in sending a surrender ultimatum to the commander of the German garrison. Even though he was short of the positions he should have occupied by this time, he hoped that the German commanders would see the hopelessness of their situation and would negotiate. The ultimatum would expire at 0900 on the next day, the 22nd.

Collins had, on the assumption that the Germans would ignore his demands, proceeded with his plans for the final assault on Cherbourg. The first phase the attack would consist of an 80-minute pummeling of the known German defenses by aircraft of the American 9th Tactical Air Command, the British 2nd Tactical Air Force and the American 9th Air Force. It was scheduled to begin at 1200hrs on the 22nd. But, as with almost every major operation in the European Theater, everything depended on the weather.

The offensive by the American forces to actually take the port of Cherbourg was to be an almost entirely Army affair. Some sources are of the opinion that the Army wanted the glory of capturing such a prestigious objective for itself and so had not requested naval gunfire support during the siege. This thesis is possible in light of the many after action reports submitted by senior Army commanders which tended to denigrate, if totally not ignore, the effect that naval gunfire had had on the entire campaign thus far. It might have been that there was a feeling amongst those same senior Army officers that it was time for the Army to receive some of the headlines that the Navy had been garnering during the initial phases of the invasion.

However, if we look at the Navy's reluctance, even on D-Day, to come within range of a single battery of German artillery at Point du

Hoc near *Omaha* beach another opinion might arise. In that case they had steadfastly maintained the position of their heavier and thus more effective units 12,000 yards off the beach. This had protected their more valuable vessels from the danger of German counter-fire, but had also required a much longer and more dangerous voyage than was necessary for the landing craft and the troops they carried. This obvious reluctance by the Navy to risk their ships in confrontations with fixed artillery ashore would seem to be a more probable reason for their lack of involvement in the action around Cherbourg.

At the very end of the operation to take Cherbourg they would make one quick hit and run bombardment sortie against the harbor's outer defenses. By that time, the action was more of a final blow to the morale of the German garrison rather than of any real assistance in the taking of the city.

During the relatively brief exchange of gunfire, several targets on shore were hit, mostly shore batteries. The Royal Navy's light cruiser GLASGOW, the American destroyers BARTON, O'BRIEN and LAFFEY, as well as the American battleship TEXAS were damaged by German counter-fire. The damage suffered by the attacking naval force during this skirmish may offer some justification of the Navy's concerns about fixed artillery positions ashore.

At 1240hrs, on the 22nd, the day of the assault on the city, the first of the Allied aircraft began their attacks. By 1300hrs American ground units were calling in reports that they were being bombed and strafed by "friendly" airplanes apparently due to identification and communication issues. The problems were in large part eventually resolved and the air attack on Cherbourg continued.

For all its flash and bang, the massive aerial assault was largely ineffective in destroying the German defenses. What it did accomplish was the almost complete disruption of the German communication system, a fact that would be both a help and a hindrance when the Americans began entering the city itself. It also had the effect of further lowering the morale of the garrison.

At 1430hrs, the American ground troops finally began advancing towards the outer defenses of Cherbourg. At the end of the day the

Americans, after heavy fighting, were still trying to penetrate those same positions.

The morning of the 23rd found the attack being resumed at 0830hrs. By that evening units of the 9th Division finally broke through the outer defensive line of the Germans and began advancing towards the city. In the post-battle evaluations, it was determined that the 9th had been by far the most effective of the three assault divisions that took part in the offensive against the port of Cherbourg. This verdict and later successes enjoyed by the 9th would help propel its commander, Major General Manton S. Eddy, to another star and a corps command by the end of the war.

This was also the day that a member of the 9th Division was awarded the unit's first Medal of Honor. The citation of Second Lieutenant John E. Butts, of the 60th Infantry Regiment, read that previously on the 14th and 16th of the month he had received wounds serious enough to warrant evacuation back to Britain, but he had refused to leave his platoon. On the 23rd, still suffering from his previous wounds, he would lead his men against a German strongpoint near Flottemanville Hague outside Cherbourg. He was critically wounded in the initial attack. He then ordered his platoon to outflank the enemy position while he alone attacked made a frontal assault. He was hit again and crawled to within 10 yards of the German defenses before he was hit yet again and was killed.

The same day that the Americans broke through his outer defenses, German garrison commander von Schlieben received a "promotion" from Berlin. He was named as the commander of the "Fortress Cherbourg", relieving Generalmajor Robert Sattler, who became his subordinate. Until then he had only been responsible for the remains of the four shattered divisions that were attempting to defend the city. Now he would have honor of commanding a fortress that was doomed to fall.

Finally on the morning of the 24th the outskirts of the city were reached. Several strong points within the city were taken before the end of the day and it was assumed by both sides that the next day would bring the final and overwhelming assault on the German defenders.

At 0730 on the morning of the 25th, a German medical officer, under a flag of truce, came through the frontline of the 9th Division. He requested plasma for his wounded and asked that the Naval Hospital near the port be spared. He was given the plasma and returned to the German lines. He carried with him a demand for the immediate surrender of the city. Soon after this, the attack resumed and it culminated with the capture of Fort du Roule, a fortification that overlooked the harbor and inner city. Heavy and intense street fighting would continue until the end of the day.

It was at Fort du Roule that First Lieutenant Carlos C. Ogden of the 79th Division would win the Medal of Honor. After his company was pinned down by German fire, he had procured a rifle and several grenades. He then proceeded to attack the enemy emplacements by himself. Even after being severely wounded, he continued his assault and succeeded in destroying a German artillery piece and two machine guns. His actions were vital in the securing of the Fort.

In a rare double, another member of the 79th was also awarded the Medal of Honor for the same action. Corporal John D. Kelly was cited for repeatedly advancing under heavy fire in order to destroy fortifications protecting the fort. Kelly was seriously wounded in the course of his attacks. He would die in November as a result of his wounds and would be awarded the Medal posthumously.

Organized resistance by the German garrison would finally end on the 26th. Von Schlieben and the Port Commander of Cherbourg, Admiral Walter Hennecke, personally surrendered, but claimed that they could not officially surrender the entire city due to destruction of the city's communication system and the inability to reach all their units that were still fighting. By the end of the day they were convinced otherwise. An official surrender ceremony was held the morning of the 27th at 1000. More than 10,000 Germans became prisoners. Apparently, they had forgotten Hitler's order that they fight to the last man and the last bullet.

Von Schlieben thought that he was rather ill-treated after his surrender, considering his rank. Although General Bradley had momentarily considered inviting the German General to dinner, he changed his mind after it was pointed out to him that an earlier capitulation by the German garrison would have saved many American lives. The tribulations of the German general would continue after he had consumed his first meal in captivity, standard Army-issue K-rations served in his farmhouse jail, which by the way had no shower. Apparently, there was no end to the barbarity of the Americans. Then to top it off, the vehicle carrying his personal belongings from Cherbourg collided with another truck and scattered his clothing all over the road. By the time it was recovered, all the medals and every piece of gold braid had disappeared at the hands of souvenir hungry American GIs.

There were still several groups of Germans holding out in smaller forts along the outer harbor, but within the next few days they would be eliminated or convinced to surrender.

The last major action on the Contentin occurred when the 9th Division was assigned the task of reducing an enemy pocket rumored to exist on Cap de la Hague to the west of Cherbourg. After locating and confirming the existence of the German formation, the 9th spent the next 4 days in heavy fighting which resulted in the capture of another 6,000 Germans.

The Allies had finally achieved one of their primary objectives of the initial invasion plan. They had control of the Contentin and its port of Cherbourg. But, having it and utilizing it were two different things.

The Allies wouldn't be able to make full use of the harbor for months. The Germans had not only destroyed all the port facilities, but had dumped thousands of contact, pressure and acoustic mines within the harbor itself. Until every mine had been accounted for, any serious use of the all-important inner harbor was impossible. The Germans had accomplished "the most complete, intensive and best planned demolition in history". This in the words of the man in charge of the cleanup, US Army Corps of Engineers Colonel A. Viney, commander of the unit responsible for restoring the harbor,

The destruction of the Cherbourg harbor was so thorough that it earned the praise of Adolf Hitler himself. He awarded the Knight's Cross to Rear Admiral Walter Hennecke; the port commander and the man responsible for the utter desolation that the Americans encountered when they entered what they had hoped would be the solution to their supply problems.

Two days after the surrender on the 29th, a mine disposal team commanded by Royal Navy Commander F. Landon began investigating the main inner harbor which had been saturated with mines. By the 13th of July they had neutralized more than 150. There were hundreds still sitting on the harbor floor awaiting a victim. The existence of those mines and the extraordinary demolition work performed by the Germans meant that it would be several months before the inner harbor could be used at anywhere near its full capacity and by that time the war would be all the way to the German border.

On July 1st a group of Royal Navy minesweepers commanded by Commodore J. Temple began clearing mines from the secondary outer harbor which would be available for limited service within a few weeks.

On July 5th USN Commodore W.A. Sullivan personally inspected the basins and quays within the inner harbor. He had been the person most responsible for the decision not to repair *Mulberry "A"* after the June 19th storm. After viewing the destruction that the Germans had wrought on the port and its facilities, he may have had second thoughts about that decision.

It wasn't until July 16th that the first Allied freighter finally entered the outer harbor. The Allies wouldn't be able to make full use of the more important inner harbor until November.

Even Cherbourg itself was somewhat of a stopgap measure. It had been an important seaport before the war, but one that had been designed mainly for the passenger trade, not that of cargo. The docking and mooring areas were far too small to handle the number of ships that would eventually be required to deliver the huge amount of supplies that the Allied armies would need if they were to fight their way out of France.

Although it was obvious to the Allied planners that Cherbourg was not going to be the end-all to their supply problems, it was hoped that it would suffice until a larger and more efficient harbor could be taken. Le Havre to the east was to be the next step. After that, Antwerp in

Belgium and Marseilles in the south of France would hopefully be the final pieces to the supply puzzle.

The ports along the Brittany coast were also to have been utilized, but as so often happens in war plans and priorities change. The American Third Army was to have taken Brest, as well as the smaller ports of St. Nazaire and L'Orient. After accomplishing this task it would then provide support for the First Army in its offensive towards Paris. Those plans were altered after the battle for Brest. The facilities at Brest were eventually captured, but the price was too high.

The German garrisons were obeying Hitler's orders to hold at all costs. Also, the port itself was found to be in such a state that it would prove to be all but useless for immediate use. The defenders had more than enough time to demolish it. It was logical to assume that the same situation could be expected at other ports that were further down the coast. The decision was then made to leave one of the Third Army's corps, the VIII under the command of General Troy Middleton, around the remaining Brittany ports to contain their garrisons. The rest of the Third Army would then join the First Army in attacking the main German forces to the east.

Middleton's command was eventually relieved by units of the American Ninth Army when that unit was activated. It then rejoined its parent organization in its offensive.

The commander of the Third Army, General George Patton, had a definite reputation for not taking a backseat to anyone when it came to action or glory. Although he was happy to finally be involved in the war again, he had never been thrilled with his support role. There were more headlines to be garnered at the sword's point than there were farther down its blade. Even before the decision to bypass the rest of the Brittany ports had been made, he was already making plans for his own war. It was well that he did, for when his Third Army was released from its supporting roll it immediately went on a tear that would have done credit to the famous "Blitzkriegs" of the German Wehrmacht in its glory days at the beginning of the war.

Unfortunately, the Patton blitzkrieg would only last until the end of August. By that date, the Third Army had advanced almost 600 kilometers. From September 1st until the middle of December it gained just 35 kilometers. The main reason for Third Army's slowdown, as well as that of the rest of the Allied Expeditionary Force, was one of logistics. It was the same problem that had created the need for the *Mulberry* concept and it wasn't going to disappear now that the Germans were retreating.

As we all know the British and Americans eventually overcame those supply issues, as well as countless others. Many must have seemed insurmountable. Many of those difficulties would arise from differences of the two nationalities. Attitudes, values, you name it, and it was different. The odds were against this unlikely alliance surviving, let alone winning the war. But they beat the odds and they beat Hitler, although it was touch and go at times, as the next chapter illustrates.

THE REST OF THE STORY

Past history naturally had much to do with national preferences concerning how to conduct the invasion and win the war. The Americans had never lost a war, so they had a rather high opinion of their own military theories. They tended to believe that once they came to grips with their enemy, it was impossible for them to lose. The way they saw it, after they made it to the beach it was on to Berlin and let's win the war by Christmas. They had the industrial might of the greatest country on the planet behind them. How could they lose?

An interesting analogy might be to compare the military thought process of the U.S. Army in 1944 to that of the Union Army in 1864. The commander of 1864 was Ulysses Grant. He wasn't a man who had much use for maneuver or subterfuge. He believed that the forces he commanded were superior in every way to those of his opposition. He would simply attack head-on, wear down his enemy and eventually over-whelm them. He had won his war using this uncomplicated and costly strategy and it had earned him the nick-name "The Butcher".

Many of the commanders of the American Army of 1944, from Army Chief of Staff George Marshall on down, had studied the campaigns of Grant since before they had become officers. It was time that might have been better spent examining those of Grant's opponent General Robert E. Lee.

Lee, as the perpetual underdog, had always been looking for a less expensive way to win a battle. If he could devise a maneuver that was a little more complicated, but might cost him fewer casualties and still win the battle, he would use it. He preferred to go around his enemy rather than over him. But, alas, he had not won his war so there must have been a flaw in his plan. Americans love a winner and Lee was an admirable loser. So Grant's way was the path they would follow.

Even an American commander like General George Patton who was famous for exploiting his enemy's flanks, as well as disregarding his own, would eventually fall victim to this "style" of warfare. When his Third Army reached the city of Metz in the Lorraine district of France he found himself reverting to the Grant form of offense.

Metz is located in an area that has seen more warfare than almost any other part of continental Europe and had been the site of almost continuous fortification building since the latter part of the 17th century. At the time of Patton's attack, it was considered by many to be the most fortified city in the most fortified part of Europe. For whatever reason, when Patton got Metz in his sights, he came down with tunnel vision. He forgot about moving around flanks and tried to bulldoze his way in.

Another instance of the American high command's preference for going through rather than around would be the case of the Huertgen Forest. Often, during the war, American generals would try to outflank strongly held enemy positions, but every once in a while, they would fall back on the costly glory of the head-on attack as they unfortunately chose to do in the Huertgen.

From September until December, the US First Army commanded by General Courtney Hodges would shove 120,000 American soldiers through what was a virtual meat grinder. They would suffer 24,000 combat casualties and lose another 9,000 to frostbite and trench foot in an utterly useless campaign.

The decision to take the Forest, rather than move around it to what should have been their real target may have been merely another case of over-confidence on the part of the Americans. But, once they had committed themselves to the fight, they compounded their error by continuing to send division after division into the deadly and useless battle rather than admitting their mistake and adjusting to the situation.

The ultimate objective of the offensive was a series of dams to the east. These dams controlled the water level on the flood plains of the Roer River further to the north. An Allied offensive on that part of the front could not take place until the Americans had secured the dams and eliminated the potential of the Germans releasing their contents and wiping out the attacking Allied forces downstream.

They could have easily maneuvered around the Forest to the north and south, isolating the German forces that held it and advanced to their real goal. In fact, that was exactly what they would end up doing the next year when they finally accomplished that mission. The Forest in itself was useless; the dams were the target. Perhaps the staffs of the US 1st Army and 12th Army Group became infatuated with a straight line on a map that went directly through the Huertgen Forest to the dams controlling the flood waters of the Roer River. After all, the shortest distance between two points is a straight line and this line directly into the heart of Germany.

Many of the members of those same staffs that made the decision to force a passage through the Huertgen were notorious for never visiting the frontlines and viewing for themselves the conditions and the terrain in which their brilliantly planned operations were to take place. If they had, there might have been a chance that reality would have set in and orders would have been changed, but they didn't visit and the orders weren't changed. Instead, thousands of American boys were uselessly sacrificed in a vain attempt to prove that the US Army could not be beaten in a head-on fight.

The all-important dams would not be taken until early the next year after the conclusion of the upcoming "Battle of the Bulge". In an interesting sidelight, several of the American divisions that were hit hardest in the Huertgen had been sent to the "quiet" area in the Ardennes to recover. When the Germans launched their surprise offensive in December, the brunt of the attack would fall on these units that were resting and rebuilding after the ill-conceived assault on the Huertgen.

On D-Day, there is no better example of this line of military thinking than the assault plan the Americans had conceived for their attack on "*Omaha*" beach. Rather than land their forces between the known German strong points, infiltrate around them and attack from their rear, they chose to land directly in front of them and take them head-on. Remind you of anyone?

When the action developed after the American 1st and 29th Divisions had landed on "*Omaha*" beach on D-Day, junior officers and non-commissioned officers of those units improvised the same tactics that should have been laid down in the initial planning by their "superiors". They located weaknesses in the German defensive line, exploited them and clawed their way to the top of the bluff behind the beach. They were then able to attack the German positions from the rear.

In keeping with this seemingly ingrained command philosophy of the American high command, it would follow that the American preference would have been to keep the solution to the supply problem as simple and uncomplicated as their battlefield strategy.

They realized that actual seaports would be needed eventually, but until those were captured the Americans preferred to land the supplies directly over the beaches as they had done so often and so effectively during the island war in the Pacific. In that theater, they had merely shuttled all that was required by the landing forces from a huge armada of transports stationed off-shore. In a situation where they were within 100 miles of an entire country that was serving as their supply depot, then so much the better. What could be easier than loading ships in Britain, moving them the relatively short distance to the Normandy coast and unloading them onto landing craft which would then move the necessities of war onto the shore?

But they had never tackled an operation of this magnitude or complexity in the Pacific. Attacking an island, no matter how large, was totally different than invading an entire continent. It was true that the Allies had used air power in the form of what was known as the "Transportation Plan" to isolate the battlefield and turn it into an island of sorts, but it would be impossible to surround and cut off the Germans in Normandy as they had done on numerous Japanese-held islands in the Pacific.

And unlike in the Pacific where counter-attacks were locally instigated by what was left of an island's defenders, in France they could count on concentrated and skillful counter-offensives made by thousands upon thousands of battle-hardened German soldiers. And if they didn't have the crucial supplies of ammunition and gasoline needed to withstand such an attack, they didn't have a chance.

The Landing Ship Tank (LST) was the linchpin of the American plan to land their supplies over the beach. The British had designed the proto-type LST in 1941, but due to the limited building capacities of their shipyards the project was transferred to the US. The LST was 327 feet long and displaced approximately 4,000 tons. It was approximately the same size as a light cruiser of the era.

Without the LST there would have been no possibility of landing sufficient supplies over an open beach. The LST, which was also known the "Large Slow Target" by many of its crews, had been designed for such a task. They were flat bottomed craft that could be run directly onto the beach and could carry an immense amount of cargo. They could be beached at high tide, unloaded during low tide and refloated at the next high tide. This procedure was known as "drying out". But, this removal of a scarce and valuable resource from the supply cycle by intentional stranding was an expense the Allies could ill afford. During the half day the LST was sitting on the beach waiting for the next high tide it could have been unloaded at a *Mulberry* pier, returned to Britain for another load and been half way back to Normandy.

The often over-looked or ignored fact was that while the LST could carry a load of more than 2,000 tons of cargo on the open sea, if they were landed directly onto the beach their capacity was limited to only 500 tons. That meant if they used a facility such as *Mulberry,* they could quadruple their cargo capacity, which makes one wonder why the idea of a prefabricated harbor was so repugnant to various members of both the American and the British Naval Commands.

Only slightly over 1,000 LSTs were built during the entire war and Allied amphibious operations around the world had been scheduled and rescheduled around the availability of these unglamorous, but almost priceless vessels. As a matter of fact, there would be a mere 236 LSTs off the invasion beaches on D-Day. Churchill himself had stated during one of the many conferences concerning *Neptune-Overlord* that "the destinies of two great empires seem to be tied to some God-damned things called LSTs".

Admiral Hall, commander of the American assault forces off *Omaha* on D-Day and one of the most vocal critics of the *Mulberry* concept, had proclaimed that with 1,000 LSTs he could land sufficient supplies over the beaches to meet the needs of the Allied armies during the initial assault phase of the invasion. The question that begs to be asked of this opinion is where was the Admiral was going to get his 1,000 LSTs. American shipyards were already building them as fast as possible and there were only a couple months until the invasion. The Allies did not enjoy the luxury of having enough time to wait for the completion of Hall's fantasy fleet.

Many British and American commanders questioned whether the US Navy was hoarding LSTs for its preferred Theater, the Pacific. There doesn't seem to be much foundation for these charges. As of June 1, 1944, there were only 102 LSTs in the entire Pacific Theater of Operations. Another 95 were in various stages of construction in the US and 25 more were located in the Mediterranean.

The supply of LSTs was so tight that when three were sunk or damaged by German S-boats off southern Britain during a training exercise called *"Operation Tiger"* special authorization from Washington had to be attained to transfer replacements from the Mediterranean.

The British themselves were to blame for many of the shortages of landing craft available for the invasion. They had continually vacillated since 1942 on a date for invading France. Every time the Americans thought they had a confirmed date they would give the construction of landing craft a higher priority. Then the British would change their minds and those priorities would revert to vessels that were considered more critical at that time. This situation, when combined with the U.S. Navy's undeniable preference for building bigger and more imposing vessels led to an almost totally unnecessary dearth of these highly critical items throughout the war.

The Americans also believed that the British had a tendency to get a little too cute with their strategy and their gadgets. The distaste exhibited by several American commanders for many British ideas and theories extended from major strategic decisions to individual weapons. Before the landings, there were many senior Americans that were of the opinion that even the soon to be highly successful deception plan "*Operation Fortitude*" was a waste of time.

They preferred to deal with the situation with a minimum of distractions. The majority of Americans seemed to think that the British were just a tad slow and methodical in all their operations. The British seemed to have no problem waiting until tomorrow if they deemed it necessary. The Americans on the other hand wanted it done yesterday. If they had had their way the Allies would have attacked Northwestern Europe in 1942 instead of committing to operations in the Mediterranean in the form of "*Operation Torch*", the invasion of North Africa.

So, when they were presented with the idea of a harbor that would be towed across the ocean it appeared to be just another example of the British wasting time and money instead of getting down to the business of ending the war as soon as possible. Many of the Americans had been in favor of a breakwater system to protect the beaches, but felt that the complicated and expensive pier arrangement was unnecessary and far too fragile to withstand weather conditions in the Channel.

An indication of this attitude was the haste which the American High Command exhibited when it decided not to repair their *Mulberry* "A" after the storm of June 19th. They had always felt that off-loading directly onto the beaches until the eventual capture of Cherbourg should have been the plan all along. When Mother Nature brought down her wrath upon *Mulberry*, as they had predicted she would, the Americans felt that they had fulfilled their obligations and could now proceed with operations as they should have been conducted all along.

The British on the other hand, had been had been fighting a war since 1939 that they had come close to losing on more than one occasion. They tended to be a little more cautious and pessimistic than the Americans. Many on the British side also considered America a somewhat junior and, most definitely, a less experienced partner. They didn't hesitate to lecture senior commanders of the US forces on the proper way to fight a war. This superiority complex, when coupled with a slight inferiority complex on the part of the Americans, had led to much friction throughout the war and would continue to do so until the end of the conflict. This might explain the attitude of many American commanders towards the *Mulberry* project. If the "Limeys" built it, it was probably more complicated and expensive than it needed to be. They would almost always favor the more direct and less complicated approach to a problem.

If the Americans preferred the hard-charging uncomplicated tactics and strategies of General Grant of the American Civil War then the British definitely leaned more towards those of his adversary General Lee, which tended to be a little more creative. But, that had not always been a trademark of British military thinking.

The British had fought the First World War like the Americans wanted to fight the Second. During the "war to end all wars" they knew they could beat the Germans, so why bother with feints, diversions and trickery. They had used the same tactics and strategies for centuries and had been very successful so why change. This arrogance had led to the stalemate on the Western Front and the hideous casualties they had suffered in countless mindless charges across the no-man's land between the German and Allied lines during that conflict.

The British Empire could ill-afford to waste the cream of its youth again just a generation later in another futile attempt to prove the superiority of English manhood. Things had to change and they did.

Fortunately, even generals can learn from their mistakes. Between the wars the British Army had decided that any maneuver or device that could possibly decrease the chances of a repeat of those horrendous losses would be taken advantage of. This philosophy in a new conflict had led to a preference for periphery operations rather than frontal assaults. It would lead to many a disagreement between them and their cousins from across the Atlantic, but it also helped provide the incentive to consider alternatives to what might be considered conventional military thinking. And you couldn't get much more unconventional than building an entire harbor and dragging it across the ocean.

There will always be divided opinions on whether or not Mulberry was worth the time and treasure expended on it. What cannot be denied is that it was one of the most unique engineering achievements completed during a time of war. Even today, 65 years after the event, the idea of building two portable harbors and then towing them across 100 miles of open sea is almost incredible. And when it's taken into account that the design, building and the placing of those harbors off a hostile shore took place in a matter of months, as compared to the years it would probably take us in the present to accomplish the same feat, it verges on the unbelievable. To have even contemplated, let alone completed, a project of this magnitude and complexity in the midst of the largest conflict in human history is more than a credit to the memory of all those involved.

Royal Navy Captain Harold Hickling, Admiral Tennant's Chief of staff and later the commander of *Mulberry "B"*, was of the opinion that *Mulberry* was only responsible for 15% of the total supplies unloaded over the beaches. General Bedell Smith, Chief of Staff to the Allied Supreme Commander General Dwight Eisenhower, in response stated "that 15% was crucial" to the success of *Overlord*. In his opinion, *Mulberry* had provided the difference between victory and defeat for the Allied Expeditionary Force when the issue was most in doubt.

The official British Report to the Combined Chiefs of Staff proclaimed that without a doubt that the invasion would "probably" have succeeded without *Mulberry*. Another "probably" they might have added to their report was that the British "probably" would never have consented to *Overlord* if a supply base other than the open beaches of Normandy had not been provided. They had procrastinated for years concerning an invasion of Northern France. If *Mulberry* hadn't supplied the extra bit of encouragement that an invasion might actually succeed, the Allies might have been committed to more operations in the Mediterranean, an invasion of Norway or possibly even to Churchill's long-cherished dream of an assault through the Balkans.

The USN's Admiral Hall, who had commanded the American assault force off *Omaha*, had never been a fan of the project. Until the end of his life, he never had a problem telling anyone who would listen that it wasn't worth all the time and energy expended on it. In his opinion as much could have accomplished by landing directly on the beach and at far less cost.

A little-known fact about the *Mulberry* concept is that a similar plan was in the works for the projected American invasion of Japan in late 1945. This is very interesting in view of the negative opinions expressed by many US Naval officers concerning *Operation Mulberry*. Possibly it wasn't such a bad idea after all.

Whatever issues you may have with the way the British fought World War II, they had their moments and *Mulberry* was definitely one of them.

APPENDIX 1

A PARTIAL LIST OF GOOSEBERRY SHIPS

Utah Beach- Gooseberry 1

BENJAMIN CONTEE-An American Liberty ship that had been torpedoed by aircraft in the Mediterranean on August 16, 1943 with the loss of 264 Italian prisoners of war. She was scuttled on June 8th.

DAVID O. SAYLOR-American freighter constructed of concrete and launched in 1943.

GEORGE S. WASSON-American Liberty, had hit a mine off Britain on January 1, 1944 and was the first ship scuttled off Utah on June 8th.

MATT W. RANSOM-American Liberty ship that had hit a mine in the Mediterranean on April 11, 1943. She was scuttled on June 8th.

WEST CHESWALD-An American vessel, 6,187 tons and launched in 1919.

WEST HONAKER- American vessel, 5376 tons and launched in 1920. Was scuttled on June 8th.

WEST NOHNO-An American vessel, 6186 tons and launched in 1919.

VICTORY SWORD- American vessel, 4,711 tons and launched 1910. Was scuttled on June 8th.

VITRUVIUS-American freighter constructed of concrete. 4,690 tons and launched in 1943.

Omaha Beach-Vierville-Saint-Laurent
Gooseberry 2

ARTEMAS WARD-American Liberty involved in a collision on March 24, 1944. She was scuttled on June 8th.

AUDACIOUS-American vessel, 7,166 tons and launched in 1913.

BAIALOIDE-American vessel, 6,476 tons and launched in 1914.

HMS CENTURION- A 32-year old British battleship that had had fought at the "Battle of Jutland".

COURAGEOUS- American vessel, 7,593 tons and launched in 1918. Was scuttled on June 8th.

FLIGHT COMMAND-American vessel, 4,190 tons and launched in 1911.

GALVESTON-American vessel, 6,171 tons and launched in 1921. Was scuttled on June 8th.

GEORGE W. CHILDS-American Liberty ship. Had ran aground on February 1, 1944. She was scuttled on June 8th.

JAMES W. MARSHALL-American Liberty ship. Had been bombed in the Mediterranean on October 14, 1943. She was scuttled on June 8th.

JAMES IREDELL-American Liberty ship. Had suffered storm damage in March 1944 in the Atlantic. Was scuttled on June 8th.

OLAMBALA-American vessel, 4,647 tons and launched in 1901.

POTTER-American vessel, 6,174 tons and launched in 1920.

WEST GRAMA-American vessel, 5,445 tons and launched in 1918. Was scuttled on June 8th.

WILSCOX-American vessel, 5,926 tons and launched in 1919. Was scuttled on June 8th.

Gold Beach-Arromanches
Gooseberry 3

ALYNBANK-British anti-aircraft auxiliary, 5,151 tons and launched 1925. Was the first ship scuttled on June 9th.

ALGHIOS SPYRIDON

ELSWICK PARK-British vessel, 4,188 tons and launched in 1920.

FLOWERGATE-British vessel, 5,166 tons and launched 1911.

GIORGIOS P. INGMAN

INNERTON-British vessel, 5,276 tons and launched in 1919.

LYNGHAUG-Norwegian vessel, 3,099 tons and launched in 1919.

MODLIN-Polish vessel, 3,587 tons and launched 1906.

NJEGOS-British vessel, 4,393 tons and launched in 1908.

PARKHAVEN-Dutch vessel, 4,803 tons and launched in 1920.

PARKLAAN-Dutch vessel, 3,869 tons and launched in 1911.

SALTERSGATE-British vessel, 3,940 tons and launched in 1924.

SIREHEI-Norwegian vessel, 3,856 tons and launched in 1907.

VINLAKE-British vessel, 3,938 tons and launched in 1913.

WINHA-British vessel, 3,313 tons and launched in 1904.

Juno Beach-Courseulles
Gooseberry 4

BELGIQUE-Belgian vessel, 4,592 tons and launched in 1902.

BENDORAN-British vessel, 5,559 tons and launched in 1910.

EMPIRE BUNTING-British vessel, 6,318 tons and launched in 1910.

EMPIRE FLAMINGO-British vessel, 5,543 tons and launched in 1920.

EMPIRE MOORHEN-British vessel, 5,628 tons and launched in 1919.

EMPIRE WATERHEN-British vessel, 6,004 tons and launched in 1920.

FORMIGNY-British vessel, 2,957 tons and launched in 1917.

MANCHESTER SPINNER-British vessel, 4,767 tons and launched in 1919.

MARIPOSA-British vessel, 3,702 tons and launched in 1914.

PANOS-British vessel, 4,914 tons and launched in 1920.

VERA RADCLIFFE-British vessel, 5,587 tons and launched in 1925.

Sword Beach-Ouistreham
Gooseberry 5

BECHEVILLE-British vessel, 4,218 tons and launched in 1924.

COURBET-French battleship. Scuttled on June 9th. She was the only block-ship that had to be towed across the Channel, the rest made it under their own power. She was actually torpedoed by the Germans while serving as a Corncob.

DOVER HILL

HMS DURBAN-A British light cruiser launched in 1919. She was scuttled on June 9th.

EMPIRE DEFIANCE-British vessel, 4,667 tons and launched in 1919.

EMPIRE TAMAR-British vessel, 6,640 tons and launched in 1907.

EMPIRE TANA-British freighter.

FORBIN-French vessel, 7,653 tons and launched in 1923.

HNLMS SUMATRA- Dutch heavy cruiser. She was scuttled on June 9th.

*Several ships were added to the breakwater at later dates, but these were the initial vessels involved.

APPENDIX 2

TIGER

Operation Tiger was one of the final training exercises involving the American 4th Infantry Division which was to assault Utah Beach in Normandy. In a prime example of how dangerous "training" can be, the losses suffered in this exercise far outstripped those suffered by the 4th in its actual landing on Utah.

It took place off Slapton Sands on the South Devon coast of Britain. Two LSTs were sunk and 6 more were damaged by German S-boats operating out of Cherbourg, France. Between 640 and 749 American soldiers and sailors were lost in this little-known incident and approximately 300 were wounded. The casualty estimates vary considerably due to the confusion that naturally occurs during a surprise night engagement. The Allies did manage to learn a few lessons from this disaster.

After this incident, rescue vessels would accompany major shipping movements, all passengers would be trained in the use of life jackets and American and British naval units would use the same radio frequencies. It's hard to believe that these seemingly common-sense requirements were not already in place but they were not.

APPENDIX 3

FORTITUDE

"Operation Fortitude" was conceived during the "Rattle" Conference at the Hollywood Hotel in Largs, Scotland on June 28, 1943. Attendees at this meeting included more than 80 admirals and generals from Britain, the U.S. and Canada. It was at this time that the beaches of Normandy were officially chosen for the return of the Allies to Continental Europe.

It was painfully obvious to those who would be in command of that invasion that an assault across open beaches in the face of a concentrated and alert German defense force would be extremely difficult, if not impossible. Thus, that defending force must be dispersed and/or distracted. The plan was to convince the Germans that the landings would take place anywhere from Norway to the Pas de Calais on the French coast, anywhere but Normandy.

They would create a fictional army of 350,000 imaginary troops in Scotland for an imaginary assault on Norway. The Germans would also be encouraged to become focused on the largely non-existent First U.S. Army Group commanded by the American General George S. Patton which was supposedly billeted in southeastern Britain near the Channel coast. The location of this fictitious unit was widely known and it was promoted to the British public as the future liberators of France by way of the Pas de Calais.

In order to help placate Patton for any ill feelings he may have had about being used as a decoy instead of being involved in the actual invasion, he had been promised command of the real-life 3rd Army when that force was activated after the successful completion of the initial landings.

Although Fortitude would not convince the German High Command that the invasion would be mounted at a specific location, it created enough doubt in their minds that they were never totally sure that any possibility could be discounted.

APPENDIX 4

RED BALL EXPRESS

The express was basically a 24-hour a day shuttle service consisting of regular cargo trucks loaded with supplies, mostly fuel carried in 5-gallon containers. They were driven on an outbound route from the Channel coast to a main depot behind the frontlines. After discharging their loads, they would proceed along another route back to the coast.

Considering the fuel burned by the trucks themselves and the time rather inefficiently expended in the effort it would seem to be a rather sad commentary on the abilities of the officers charged with keeping the Allied armies moving towards Germany.

In an interesting illustration of American society at the time, the majority of the truck drivers were Black. At the time, they weren't considered competent enough for the combat branches, so in large part they were relegated to service duties such as stevedore or truck driving.

www.ingramcontent.com/pod-product-compliance
Lightning Source LLC
LaVergne TN
LVHW041810060526
838201LV00046B/1197